More Wok Cookery

ANOTHER BESTSELLING VOLUME FROM HPBOOKS

Publisher: Bill and Helen Fisher; Executive Editor: Rick Bailey; Editorial Director: Veronica Durie; Editor: Carroll Latham; Art Director: Don Burton; Book Design: George Haigh; Food Stylist: Janet Pitman; Photography: George de Gennaro Studios

NOTICE: The information contained in this book is true and complete to the best of our knowledge. All recommendations are made without guarantees on the part of the author or HPBooks. The author and publisher disclaim all liability incurred in connection with the use of this information.

Published by HPBooks
P.O. Box 5367, Tucson, AZ 85703   602/888-2150
ISBN 0-89586-138-0
Library of Congress Catalog Card Number: 82-81010
©1982 Fisher Publishing Inc. Printed in U.S.A.

Cover: Mediterranean Chicken, page 127.

Vegetables

1. Green onions
2. Red onions
3. Bok choy
4. Eggplant
5. Green cabbage
6. Red cabbage
7. Mushrooms
8. Broccoli
9. Snow or Sugar Snap peas
10. Tomatoes

For Your Wok

11. Zucchini squash	16. Green beans	21. Enoki mushrooms
12. Asparagus	17. Cauliflower	22. Crookneck squash
13. Chinese cabbage	18. Yellow onion	23. Gingerroot
14. Corn on the cob	19. Carrots	24. Garlic
15. Red radishes	20. Green peppers	25. Pattypan squash

wok in hot water. Dry it thoroughly inside and outside with paper towels or a cloth. It is especially important to dry the heat control socket. When you are sure the socket is completely dry, insert the temperature control and heat the wok to 250F (120C). Use paper towels to rub a teaspoon of peanut oil or vegetable oil other than corn oil over the inside surface of the hot wok. Hold the paper towels with tongs, if necessary.

Conventional steel woks with non-stick interior finishes are seasoned and cleaned like an electric wok.

Cleaning wok accessories is no different than cleaning any cooking tool. Just wash them in hot soapy water. Metal racks and the wok ring base can be washed in a dishwasher. The aluminum dome lid should be washed by hand and wiped immediately to keep it shiny.❖

Wok Cooking Methods

All the delicious recipes in this book are prepared in a wok by quick and easy Oriental cooking methods. Use the method that best suits the food to be prepared.

Stir-Fry—to use a metal wok spatula or a wooden spoon to toss, lift and stir diced, shredded or chopped food in a wok over high heat. Use only enough oil to keep food from sticking to the wok. Cook until all ingredients are crisp-tender. Stir-frying is easy and the results spectacular.

Most instructions for stir-frying say that because the actual cooking is so fast, you must have everything sliced, diced and chopped ahead of time. This is the best way, of course, but somehow the impression is given that if even one ingredient is forgotten, all is lost. Not at all.

Take the wok off the heat and quickly toss the ingredients to cool them and slow the cooking process. If the forgotten ingredient must be chopped, or even if you must send someone to the corner store, it's still no catastrophe. Simply transfer the partially cooked food to a platter until you are ready to continue cooking. Stir-fry the previously missing ingredient to the degree of doneness desired, add the partially cooked food and proceed as though you had never been inter-rupted. Your dish might be just a bit overcooked, but few people will be aware of it. Flavors will be as delicious as if there had been no delay.

Ceil Dyer uses her wok at home and finds it especially useful when she entertains. Her friends and neighbors are intrigued by the savory aroma of foods that come from her kitchen.

A graduate of Louisiana State University, Ceil was a New York food publicist for wine and food companies for a number of years. She later wrote a wine and food column featuring quick gourmet entertaining. Now, in a lovely rural setting, most of her time is spent developing new and exciting recipes.

Ceil has authored more than 30 cookbooks. One is the bestseller, *Wok Cookery*, which has over one-million copies in print. In *More Wok Cookery*, she has included over 200 different and delicious recipes for the wok.❖

Stir-frying is a way of cooking that can be used as successfully for one vegetable or meat as for an assortment of foods. It can also be used to prepare recipes from many different cuisines. For example, Normandy Chicken, page 127, is a French classic that tastes even better when stir-fried in a wok than when prepared in a flat-bottom sauté pan. The chicken is cooked before it has time to steam and become dry.

Water chestnuts, bamboo shoots and snow peas are often used to add variety and crisp texture to stir-fry dishes. You can use other equally delicious foods to obtain the same fabulous results. For a change, use crisp cubes of sun chokes or crisp, young radishes instead of water chestnuts. Sun chokes have the same nut-like quality. Instead of frozen snow peas, use your own garden-fresh Sugar Snap peas. Small turnips are an excellent substitute for canned bamboo shoots. Instead of the usual plain white rice, serve a rice seasoned with curry powder or turmeric, or serve a stir-fried mixture over noodles, hot cooked bulgar, toasted corn bread squares or French bread. To sum up, you can be selective with stir-frying. Use what's on hand, what pleases you and your guests or family.

Be creative. It's indeed a great way to cook.

Deep-Fry—to cook food completely submerged in hot oil. You have probably deep-fried food before now, but have you deep-fried Oriental-style in a wok? If not, you will be pleasantly surprised to find it's easier and less expensive than frying Occidental-style.

Less oil is needed in a wok, yet its generous circumference allows more food to be fried at one time. The food is almost always cut to medium or small pieces. It is often marinated and may be precooked. Therefore, frying time is faster than usual. Foods are cooked so fast, they are non-greasy. The extra bonus is that almost all deep-fried wok dishes can be prepared ahead and reheated or served at room temperature. Deep-fried foods may be stored in your freezer to reappear whenever you need something really special to serve.

How to Stir-Fry Food

1/Lift and stir diced, shredded or chopped food over high heat. Cook vegetables only until crisp-tender.

2/Stir-fry longer-cooking foods first. Add foods that require very little heating just before serving.

Steam—to cook by moist steam on a rack in a wok. It was not until after I started cooking in my wok that I got over my misunderstanding of steaming. I somehow confused this method with limp, over-cooked and tasteless steam-table fare. But after tasting wok-steamed food, I realized how wrong I had been.

The best way to cook foods to preserve their fresh flavor and natural color is to steam them in a wok. Steamed foods retain more nutrients than foods cooked by any other cooking method. Vitamins B and C, as well as all minerals, are water soluble and end up in cooking water unless the food is steamed. Equally important, steamed food tastes positively marvelous!

When you prepare tender, succulent Fillet of Sole Florentine, page 76, you will know what I'm talking about. I become hungry just writing about it. Meringue desserts—incredibly light, yet rich and flavorful—are my favorites. Pink-Cloud Meringue Cake, page 142, is just such a dessert. The batter is spooned into a Bundt pan, then steamed on a rack in a wok. And it's as pretty as a picture. After you try these recipes, I know you'll become as enthusiastic as I am about steamed food.

To steam properly requires only a rack—either one made especially for your wok or a cake rack. It should be about 2 inches smaller in circumference than the top of your wok. Pour water into the wok until it is 1 inch below the rack. Place the wok over medium heat and bring the water to a gentle boil. This will produce steam, but the water won't boil up into the food. Place food directly on the rack or in a baking dish or ovenproof plate on the rack. Cover your wok with its high-dome lid and the cooking time begins. Because steam-cooking is often fast, it's best to watch the timing. Be careful not to overcook foods. Steamed fish, for instance, takes only minutes to reach perfection. Follow the times given in the recipes, but check the food one or two minutes before the specified time has elapsed. Steam heat is variable, or fluctuates, and foods may cook faster or slower than expected.❖

How to Steam Food

1/Steam large pieces of food by placing them on a rack over gently boiling water. See chart on page 34.

2/Steam small pieces of food in a dish or on a steaming rack.

Shopping Strategy

Have you shopped your supermarket lately? It's not a ridiculous question. I don't mean shopped *at*—dashed through to grab the same items you buy week after week. I mean *shopped*— taken time to browse, to walk leisurely down aisles and examine what's new on the shelves. If not, you might find it well worth your time.

Supermarkets have changed. In almost every community you will find at least one supermarket that is what I call a *super-supermarket*. Such a market usually has a splendid deli department with a number of fine, imported and domestic meats and cheeses. You may also find a nice bakery and a well-stocked gourmet section. It also has the largest and best produce department in town. Here's where you find most of those items that, until recently, could only be found at ethnic markets, health food or specialty stores.

Many of the so-called *foreign* ingredients in this book were purchased at my local supermarket. These ingredients are staples in my kitchen. I don't use them just once for an exotic dish, but many times for many different recipes. You are probably already familiar with most of them. The following shopping list includes some foreign foods and some equally important alternatives that you can use as substitutes.

Oriental Vegetables For Wok Cookery

Bamboo Shoots—Crisp and chewy bamboo shoots add texture to soups, stews, casseroles and stir-fry dishes. Canned bamboo shoots can be found in most supermarkets. **Substitute:** sun chokes or jícama. Both retain the same crisp quality when cooked, and have an added dimension of juicy, fresh flavor.

Bean Sprouts—Fresh sprouts are crunchy, tender and uniquely flavorful. Perfect for use in stir-fries, they also make a fine addition to salads, sandwiches and soups. Fresh sprouts are far superior to canned sprouts. Make sure they are fresh when you buy them. Shop for sprouts that are clear and white with pale-green tails. Rinse them in cold water before using. With dried mung beans on hand, bean sprouts are easy to grow in your own kitchen. See How to Sprout Mung Beans, page 55.

Chinese Cabbage—Two varieties of Chinese cabbage are called for in my recipes.

Bok choy has broad white celery-like stalks and deep green leaves. It has a crisp-tender texture and mild, sweet flavor. If you hesitate buying bok choy because it is more than you can use for a single stir-fried dish, consider using it in salads. Shred and dress it as you would cole slaw. Or stir it into soup or stew just before serving. **Substitute:** romaine lettuce.

Siew choy is called *Chinese cabbage* throughout this book. It is a large, oval-shaped light-green cabbage with crinkly, close-fitting leaves. This elongated cabbage is more delicately flavored than Western cabbage, yet it can be cooked in the same way. It's a natural for stir-frying, yet can be used in salads. You can stuff and serve the inner leaves as you would celery. **Substitute:** young, very green Savoy cabbage.

Daikon—*Dai* is Japanese for large and *kon* means root. This crisp vegetable looks like a huge white radish. It can be eaten raw or cooked. **Substitute:** 4 or 5 small white radishes for each daikon.

Enoki Mushrooms—These creamy white, long-stemmed Japanese mushrooms with an outer-space look have a mild flavor and crisp texture. They are a beautiful last-minute addition to stir-fried dishes or a garnish for almost any food.

Gingerroot—A pungent and aromatic, but subtle, seasoning root to flavor just about any dish. **Substitute:** preserved or candied ginger, rinsed to remove excess sugar.

Snow Peas—Buy these lovely, crisp, green, edible pea pods fresh when you can find them, but frozen pea pods are also superb. **Substitute:** Sugar Snap peas give you the same delectable, garden-fresh taste.

Water Chestnuts—This water-grown vegetable with a nutty, sweet flavor can now be found fresh

Appetizers & Buffet Fare

Do you like to give parties but can't afford it? Think again. Here are recipes that are affordable as well as festive. With planning, you can give the best parties in town.

You don't have time? Think again. Almost everyone has time to do some pleasurable cooking. Many of the recipes in this chapter can be made days or weeks ahead and frozen. You'll be ready to entertain even on very short notice. Preparing ahead lets you be a guest at your own party.

If you don't have a large assortment of party equipment, plan a finger-food buffet. All you need are three or four large bowls or platters for the food, plus a few small bowls for dipping sauces. Use paper napkins if you like. They do nicely and come in a variety of designs and colors.

With the help of a wok, you can serve really splendid food and at the same time be with your friends—not slaving away in the kitchen. Let your guests help prepare and serve from the wok. It's fun for all.

The following three ideas will help you entertain with ease:

Buffet for a Crowd

Let the number of guests determine the number of dishes you prepare. Three dishes will do nicely for eight people. Add another dish for every four or more guests. Do your cooking two or three weeks before the party. Make and freeze one or two things at a time. Reheat and place the food on the table before your guests arrive. Then stay with your guests and have a good time.

Dinner Party for 4 or 6

For a first course, serve an assortment of cocktail-size egg rolls with a predinner drink in the living room. Then prepare one stir-fry dish at the table in an electric wok or a conventional wok over a portable burner. Arrange all ingredients on the table before your guests arrive. For dessert, serve coffee and rich miniature chocolates. Then bask in well-deserved compliments to the chef.

Informal Get-Together

Make it a beer or wine party and have a big bowl of Sesame Crisps, page 28, on the table. Prepare one make-ahead finger-food such as Olive-Stuffed Meatballs Cuban-Style, page 14, or Curried Turkey Bites, page 15, and a salad. Let guests help themselves. See pages 40 to 47 for salad ideas. With everything prepared ahead, you can relax and enjoy.

Olive-Stuffed Meatballs Cuban-Style

Spicy hot meatballs with a surprise stuffing, served in a zippy tomato sauce.

3/4 lb. ground lean beef
1/2 lb. ground lean pork
1/2 cup dry breadcrumbs
1 egg
2 tablespoons water
1/4 teaspoon garlic salt
1/2 teaspoon salt
1/4 teaspoon black pepper
46 to 48 small whole pimiento-stuffed
  green olives

1/2 cup oil
1 tablespoon oil
1 large green pepper, cut in 1/4-inch pieces
1 large onion, coarsely chopped
1 (8-oz.) can tomato sauce
1/4 cup dry sherry
1/2 cup sliced pimiento-stuffed
  green olives
6 cups hot cooked rice, if desired

In a large bowl, combine beef, pork, breadcrumbs, egg, water, garlic salt, salt and black pepper. Shape mixture into 46 to 48 meatballs, 1-1/2 inches in diameter. Occasionally dip your hands in cold water to keep meat mixture from sticking. Insert 1 whole olive into center of each meatball. Shape meat to enclose olive completely; set aside. Heat 1/2 cup oil in wok over medium heat. Fry meatballs in hot oil, a few at a time, until browned on all sides, 2 to 3 minutes. Drain cooked meatballs on paper towels. Pour oil from wok. Wipe with paper towels. Heat 1 tablespoon oil in wok over medium heat. Add green pepper and onion. Stir-fry until crisp-tender, 1 to 2 minutes. Reduce heat to medium-low. Pour in tomato sauce and sherry. Add drained meatballs. Simmer 15 minutes, stirring occasionally. Stir in sliced olives. Stirring occasionally, simmer 2 to 3 minutes longer. Serve as appetizers with wooden or plastic picks for spearing, or as a main course over rice. Makes 46 to 48 meatballs.

Shahi Kafta   Photo on page 13.

North Indian lamb meatballs on skewers—party fare and very different.

2 tablespoons boiling water
1/4 teaspoon saffron threads
1 lb. ground lean lamb
2 tablespoons all-purpose flour
1 egg white, slightly beaten
1-1/2 teaspoons salt

2 tablespoons curry powder
2 tablespoons lemon juice
2 tablespoons plain yogurt
1/2 cup all-purpose flour
Oil for deep-frying
Lemon wedges

Pour boiling water into a medium bowl. Stir saffron threads into water until dissolved. Add lamb, 2 tablespoons flour, egg white, salt, curry powder, lemon juice and yogurt. Mix thoroughly. Shape into 1-1/2-inch balls. Pour 1/2 cup flour into a pie plate. Roll meatballs in flour. Shake off excess flour; set aside. Pour oil for deep-frying into wok until 1-1/2 inches deep in center. Heat oil to 375F (190C). Add a fourth of the meatballs. Fry 3 to 5 minutes, turning at least once to brown evenly. Use a slotted spoon to lift cooked meatballs from wok. Drain on paper towels. Repeat with remaining meatballs. Arrange 3 or 4 meatballs on each of 8 skewers. Serve with lemon wedges. Makes 24 to 32 meatballs or 8 appetizer servings.

On previous page: center: Sesame Shrimp Chips, page 17; clockwise from right: Cocktail Spareribs, page 27, Shahi Kafta, above, Sesame Crisps, page 28, Avery Island Shrimp Dip, page 137.

Curried Turkey Bites

Rich bite-size ground-turkey balls. Sinfully delicious.

1 lb. frozen ground turkey, thawed
1/2 cup fine dry breadcrumbs
1/2 cup dairy sour cream
1 teaspoon salt
1/4 teaspoon white pepper

1 teaspoon curry powder
2 or 3 drops hot pepper sauce
1 cup fine dry breadcrumbs
Oil for deep-frying
Lemon wedges

In a large bowl, combine turkey, 1/2 cup breadcrumbs, sour cream, salt, white pepper, curry powder and hot pepper sauce. Shape into 1-inch balls. Pour 1 cup breadcrumbs into a pie plate. Roll meatballs in breadcrumbs; set aside. Pour oil for deep-frying into wok until 1-1/2 inches deep in center. Heat oil to 350F (175C). Fry meatballs, 6 to 8 at a time, until browned on all sides, 2 to 3 minutes. Drain on paper towels. Serve with lemon wedges. Makes 24 to 26 meatballs.

Oriental Chicken Appetizer

These flavorful strips of chicken are low in calories.

2 chicken breast halves, skinned, boned
1 garlic clove, minced
1/2 teaspoon salt
1/2 cup Chicken Broth, page 134, or
   Vegetable Broth, page 133

Oriental Sauce, see below
Lettuce leaves

Oriental Sauce:
3 tablespoons soy sauce
1 teaspoon Oriental sesame oil
1 tablespoon honey

2 tablespoons dry sherry
1 teaspoon freshly grated gingerroot
2 tablespoons minced chives

Lay chicken breasts on a flat surface. Flatten by striking with side of heavy cleaver or rolling pin. Place in a shallow 1-quart glass baking dish. Sprinkle with garlic and salt. Pour broth around chicken; set aside. Place a rack in wok. Pour water into wok until 1 inch below rack. Bring water to a gentle boil over medium heat. Place dish on rack. Cover wok. Steam 20 to 25 minutes until breast is tender when pierced with a fork. Cool slightly, then refrigerate chicken in broth until chilled, about 30 minutes. Prepare Oriental Sauce; set aside. To serve, drain off marinade from chicken. Slice cooked chicken into 2'' x 1'' strips. Add to Oriental Sauce. Toss with 2 forks until chicken is coated. Arrange lettuce leaves on a small platter. Spoon coated chicken strips onto lettuce leaves. Serve immediately. Makes 6 to 8 appetizer servings.

Oriental Sauce:
Combine all ingredients in a medium bowl; blend well. Makes about 1/2 cup.

Occidental Egg Rolls

Oriental egg-roll wrappers with deliciously different Occidental fillings.

12 egg-roll wrappers
Cheese Filling, below, Crab Filling
 or Chili-Beef Filling, page 17
Oil for deep frying

Place 1 egg-roll wrapper on a flat surface with 1 corner pointing toward you. Spoon 3 to 4 tablespoons filling on center of egg-roll wrapper. Fold corner closest to you over filling, tucking point under filling. Fold left and right corners over filling, overlapping at center. Gently press to flatten slightly. Dip your fingers in cold water and brush them over upper corner of wrapper. Roll egg roll away from you and onto dampened corner. Cover filled egg rolls with a damp towel until ready to fry. If egg rolls will be held 30 to 60 minutes before frying, arrange on a platter, cover with plastic wrap and refrigerate until ready to fry. To fry egg rolls, pour oil for deep-frying into wok until 1-1/2 inches deep in center. Heat to 350F (175C). Use tongs to lower 3 or 4 egg rolls into hot fat. Turning once, fry 3 to 4 minutes until golden brown and crisp. Drain on paper towels. Repeat with remaining egg rolls. Serve hot or at room temperature. Egg rolls may be cooked, covered and refrigerated. Except for cheese-filled egg rolls, they may also be frozen. To freeze, arrange cooked egg rolls on a baking sheet. Place in freezer until frozen, about 2 hours. Place frozen egg rolls in a freezer container with a tight-fitting lid. Store in freezer up to 3 weeks. To reheat and recrisp egg rolls: Preheat oven to 350F (175C). Arrange rolls on a baking sheet. Bake refrigerated rolls 10 to 15 minutes and frozen rolls 20 to 25 minutes. Makes 12 egg rolls.

Cheese Filling for Egg Rolls

Prepare this mellow cheese filling ahead, then use in Occidental Egg Rolls, above.

3 tablespoons butter
1/4 cup all-purpose flour
1 cup hot milk (95F, 35C)
1 cup shredded sharp Cheddar cheese (4 oz.)

1/4 teaspoon salt
1/8 teaspoon pepper
1 drop hot pepper sauce
2 egg yolks, slightly beaten

Grease an 11" x 7" glass baking dish; set aside. Melt butter in a large saucepan over low heat. Stir in flour. Cook and stir 1 minute. Using a whisk, quickly stir in hot milk. Cook and stir until mixture is smooth and thick. Add cheese, salt, pepper and hot pepper sauce. Stir until cheese is melted. Cool slightly. Quickly stir in egg yolks until blended. Pour into prepared dish. Cover and refrigerate 2 to 3 hours or until mixture is cold and firm. Use about 3 tablespoons for each egg roll. Makes about 2-1/2 cups or enough filling for 12 egg rolls.

How to Make Thai Stuff

1/Cut cartilage between wing sections. Scrape me
skin toward wing tip. Twist bones and remove.

Pork Filling for (

Mango chutney adds special flavor.

1/2 lb. ground lean pork
1 garlic clove, minced
1/2 cup finely chopped water chestn
   sun chokes
1 tablespoon minced chives
2 tablespoons finely chopped chutn
   2 tablespoons orange marmalade

Cook ground pork in wok over me
spoon to break up meat. Place cook
ing ingredients. Makes enough fillin

Crab Filling for Egg Rolls

Delectable, yet not expensive. Combining crab and fish fillets is the secret.

1 lb. sole or flounder fillets
1/2 lb. crab
3/4 cup finely chopped water chestnuts or
   sun chokes

2 green onions, finely chopped
2 tablespoons chili sauce
1 tablespoon soy sauce
1 egg, slightly beaten

Chop fish fillets and crab with a sharp knife or cleaver or in food processor until minced. In a large bowl, combine minced fish, crab and remaining ingredients. Use about 1/4 cup filling for each egg roll. Makes about 3 cups or enough filling for 12 egg rolls.

Chili-Beef Filling for Egg Rolls

A blend of Mexican seasonings gives a Southwest flavor to egg rolls.

1 tablespoon oil
1 lb. ground lean beef
1 medium onion, chopped
1 garlic clove, finely chopped
1/2 teaspoon dried leaf oregano, crushed

1/2 teaspoon ground cumin
1 teaspoon salt
1 teaspoon chili powder
1/2 cup ketchup

Heat oil in wok over medium heat. Add beef, onion and garlic. Stir-fry until meat is no longer pink, 4 to 5 minutes. Stir in remaining ingredients. Cool to room temperature. Use about 2-1/2 tablespoons filling for each egg roll. Makes 2 cups or enough filling for 12 egg rolls.

Sesame Shrimp Chips   Photo on page 13.

Crispy, crunchy chips made from shrimp.

12 jumbo shrimp
1/3 cup cornstarch
Oil for deep-frying

1 tablespoon Oriental sesame oil
Salt to taste
Avery Island Shrimp Dip, page 137

Shell shrimp; remove veins and tails. Generously sprinkle both sides of cleaned shrimp with cornstarch. Place on a flat surface. Using a rolling pin or meat mallet, lightly pound each shrimp until flattened. Add more cornstarch as needed. Gently roll each shrimp with rolling pin until 1/8 inch thick. Cut each shrimp in half. Pour oil for deep-frying into wok until 1-1/2 inches deep in center. Add sesame oil. Heat oil to 350F (175C). Fry shrimp pieces, a few at a time, until crisp, about 2 minutes. Turn once. Drain on paper towels. Sprinkle cooked shrimp chips with salt to taste. Serve at room temperature with Avery Island Shrimp Dip. Makes 24 chips.

Thai Stuffed Ch

Sensational, positively sensational!

24 chicken wings
Pork Filling, page 19,
   Sausage Filling, below, or
   Spinach-Cheese Filling, page 2(
1 cup all-purpose flour
1 teaspoon salt

Holding a chicken wing in both h
Spread chicken wing open on a fla
cartilage to separate 2 larger sectic
with remaining chicken wings. Re
another use. Remove bone from
tions. Do not cut off wing tip. Sc
bones until bones can be removec
Use a small spoon or your fingers
gers to push filling all the way to
pie plate. Pour breadcrumbs into
Roll filled wings in flour mixture
wings until cold, about 1 hour. Pc
Heat oil to 350F (175C). Fry 4 o
paper towels. Serve hot or at roo
appetizers.

Batter-Fried Mini Drums

Special marinade adds superb flavor to this Oriental favorite.

24 chicken wings
1/4 cup honey
1/4 cup soy sauce
1 garlic clove, crushed
1 (1-inch) cube gingerroot, crushed
1 cup all-purpose flour

1/2 teaspoon salt
2 eggs, slightly beaten
1 cup club soda
Oil for deep-frying
Sweet & Sour Sauce, page 139

Holding a chicken wing in both hands, flex 2 larger sections back and forth to break cartilage. Spread chicken wing open on a flat surface. Use a sharp knife or cleaver to cut through skin and cartilage to separate 2 larger sections. Leave as much skin as possible on wing tip section. Repeat with remaining chicken wings. Reserve middle and wing tip sections for Thai Stuffed Chicken Wings, page 18, or another use. Use a small sharp knife to cut cartilage loose from end of bone. Holding drumstick portion in your hand, push meat and skin to top of bone. Shape into a compact ball. Arrange mini-drums in an 8-inch square glass baking dish. In a small bowl, blend honey and soy sauce. Pour over chicken. Add garlic and ginger; set aside. Place a rack in wok. Pour water into wok until 1 inch below rack. Bring water to a gentle boil over medium heat. Place baking dish on rack. Cover wok. Steam 20 to 25 minutes, turning chicken drums in honey mixture several times. Cool to room temperature. Pour water from wok. Wipe wok dry with paper towels. In a medium bowl, combine flour, salt, eggs and club soda. Beat until batter is smooth; set aside. Pour oil for deep-frying into wok until 1-1/2-inches deep in center. Heat oil to 350F (175C). Drain liquid from baking dish. Dip each chicken drum in batter. Lift from batter and swirl over bowl briefly to drain. Gently lower into hot oil. Fry 3 or 4 at a time until golden brown on all sides, 2 to 3 minutes. Serve hot or at room temperature with Sweet & Sour Sauce for dipping. Makes 24 appetizers.

Sausage Fillin

Because of the spices in the sausag

1/2 lb. breakfast sausage
1 small onion, finely chopped
1 garlic clove, minced
1 celery stalk, finely chopped
1/4 teaspoon ground marjoran

Stir-fry sausage in wok over
wooden spoon to break up pie
Pour all but about 2 tablespor
thyme. Stir-fry until onion is s
mixture cool to room temper
Makes enough filling for 24 Tl

Spinach-Cheese Filling for Chicken Wings

Spicy enough to be interesting. Also use in won tons or egg rolls.

1 (10-oz.) pkg. frozen chopped spinach,
   thawed
1/2 cup ricotta cheese (2 oz.)
3 tablespoons grated Parmesan cheese
1 egg

1/2 teaspoon salt
1/4 teaspoon pepper
1/4 teaspoon Italian seasoning
1/2 cup fine dry breadcrumbs

Press thawed spinach between your hands until all moisture is removed and spinach feels dry. Spread out on a flat surface. Use a sharp knife to chop fine. In a medium bowl, combine chopped spinach and remaining ingredients. Makes enough filling for 24 Thai Stuffed Chicken Wings, page 18.

How to Make Batter-Fried Mini Drums

1/Holding a chicken wing in both hands, flex larger sections back and forth to break cartilage. Cut apart.

2/Holding drumstick portion in your hand, push meat and skin to top of bone. Shape into a compact ball.

Sesame Stir-Fried Mushrooms

Easy, elegant and unusual. Low calorie too!

3 tablespoons sesame seeds
2 tablespoons peanut or vegetable oil
1/4 teaspoon Oriental sesame oil

1/2 lb. small mushrooms
1 tablespoon soy sauce

Place wok over medium heat. Add sesame seeds. Stir-fry until lightly browned and fragrant. Add peanut or vegetable oil and sesame oil. Increase heat to high. Add mushrooms. Stir-fry until crisp-tender. Stir in soy sauce. Serve hot with wooden or plastic picks for spearing. Mushrooms can be made ahead and reheated. Reheat 10 minutes in a preheated 350F (175C) oven. Makes 4 to 6 servings.

Western Won Tons

Big enough to take two bites and just right to serve with cocktails, beer or wine.

24 won ton skins
Spinach & Ham Filling, below, or
Feta & Broccoli Filling, opposite

Oil for deep frying
Chinese Mustard or Sweet & Sour Sauce,
page 139, or soy sauce

Place 1 won ton skin on a flat surface with 1 corner pointing toward you. Spoon about 1 teaspoon filling on side of center closest to you. Fold corner closest to you over filling. With a pastry brush or your fingers, lightly brush water on 3 remaining corners. Fold right and left corners over filled portion. Roll won ton away from you, jelly-roll fashion. Repeat with remaining skins and filling. Pour oil for deep-frying into wok until 1-1/2 inches deep in center. Heat oil to 375F (190C). Fry 4 or 5 won tons at a time in hot oil until lightly browned, 3 to 4 minutes. Drain on paper towels. Serve warm or at room temperature. To serve, dip won tons into Chinese Mustard, Sweet & Sour Sauce or soy sauce. Cooked won tons may be frozen in a single layer on a baking sheet. When firm, pack and store in an airtight storage bag or a freezer container with a tight-fitting lid. Use within 3 months. To reheat frozen won tons, arrange on a baking sheet. Reheat in a preheated 350F (175C) oven 20 to 30 minutes. Makes 24 won tons.

Spinach & Ham Filling for Won Tons

Tasty and pretty.

1 (10-oz.) pkg. frozen spinach, thawed
1 tablespoon oil
1 garlic clove, minced
1 small onion, finely chopped
1/2 cup slivered cooked ham

1/2 cup pot cheese, farmer's cheese, or
drained small-curd cottage cheese (4 oz.)
2 tablespoons dairy sour cream
1 teaspoon salt

Press thawed spinach between your hands until all moisture is removed and spinach feels dry. Place in a medium bowl; set aside. Heat oil in wok over medium-high heat. Add garlic and onion. Stir-fry until onion is soft, 1 to 2 minutes. Cool slightly. Scrape cooked garlic, onion and oil into bowl with spinach. Stir in remaining ingredients. Makes enough filling for 24 Western Won Tons.

Tip

If sliced black Greek olives are not available in your supermarket, cut the fruit from the pits of unsliced olives.

Indonesian Twice-Fried Chicken

Chefs claim chicken has a better flavor with the bone left in.

1 (2-1/2-lb.) chicken	1/4 teaspoon ground cloves
1 garlic clove	1 teaspoon sugar
1 (1-inch) cube gingerroot or	1 teaspoon salt
2 teaspoons ground ginger	1-1/4 cups cornstarch
2 green onions	1 egg, beaten
3 tablespoons soy sauce	Oil for deep-frying
2 tablespoons dry sherry	Indonesian Dipping Sauce, if desired,
2 teaspoons Oriental sesame oil	page 138
2 teaspoons coarsely ground black pepper	Sweet & Sour Hoisin Sauce, if desired,
1/2 teaspoon crushed dried hot red pepper	page 135
1/4 teaspoon ground cinnamon	

Use a sharp, heavy cleaver or knife to cut chicken in half through breast bone. Cut out center backbone. Cut through joints to separate wings, drumsticks and thighs from chicken. Cut wings at joints, making 3 pieces from each wing. With cleaver, chop bone from end of each leg. Reserve backbone, wing tips and ends of leg bones to make broth or soup. Chop meaty parts of legs in half crosswise. Chop each thigh in half crosswise. Chop each half breast crosswise, making 4 pieces from each. Set chicken aside. Use the side of a cleaver or large knive to crush garlic, gingerroot, if used, and green onions. In a large non-metal bowl, combine crushed garlic, ginger and green onions. Add soy sauce, sherry, sesame oil, black pepper, red pepper, cinnamon, cloves, sugar and salt. Add chicken pieces. Toss to coat evenly. Marinate 1 to 2 hours at room temperature, or 6 to 8 hours in refrigerator. Turn chicken several times in marinade. Pour cornstarch into a pie plate; set aside. Use a slotted spoon to remove garlic, ginger and onion from marinade. Stir egg into chicken mixture. Toss to coat evenly. Drain slightly. Roll each marinated piece of chicken in cornstarch. Shake off excess cornstarch. Pour oil for deep-frying into wok until 1-1/2 inches deep in center. Heat oil to 350F (175C). Fry coated chicken pieces, 4 or 5 at a time, in hot oil until tender, 9 to 12 minutes. Drain on paper towels. Add oil until 1-1/2 inches deep in center of wok. Heat oil to 375F (190C). Fry chicken a second time for 1 minute or until golden brown and crisp. Serve hot or at room temperature with individual bowls of Indonesian Dipping Sauce or Sweet & Sour Hoisin Sauce, if desired. Makes 8 to 10 servings.

Feta & Broccoli Filling for Won Tons

Feta is a salty Greek cheese.

1 (10-oz.) pkg. frozen chopped broccoli	1/2 cup finely crumbled feta cheese
Unsalted water	3 tablespoons fine dry breadcrumbs
2 tablespoons butter	1 egg yolk
1 garlic clove, minced	

Cook broccoli in unsalted water according to package directions. Drain thoroughly. Pat dry with paper towels. Place in a medium bowl; set aside. In a small skillet, melt butter over low heat. Add garlic. Stirring occasionally, cook until soft but not browned, about 1 minute. Cool slightly. Scrape cooked garlic and butter into bowl with broccoli. Stir in remaining ingredients. Makes enough filling for 24 Western Won Tons, opposite.

Beef Lettuce Rolls

Savory filling rolled in crisp lettuce leaves.

1 head romaine or other large-leaf lettuce
2 tablespoons finely chopped chutney
1 tablespoon brown sugar
1 tablespoon cornstarch
1 tablespoon hoisin sauce
1 tablespoon soy sauce
1 tablespoon white wine vinegar
3/4 cup Quick Beef Broth, page 133,
   Chicken Broth, page 134, or
   Vegetable Broth, page 133

2 or 3 drops hot pepper sauce
2 tablespoons oil
1 garlic clove, minced
1 small mild red onion, chopped
1 lb. ground lean beef
1/2 cup slivered water chestnuts or
   sun chokes
1/2 cup raisins
1 tablespoon crushed dried hot red pepper
1 cup fresh bean sprouts

Cut out lettuce core and gently separate leaves. Rinse under cold running water. Arrange 16 to 20 leaves on a large plate or platter. Refrigerate until ready to serve. In a small bowl, combine chutney, brown sugar, cornstarch, hoisin sauce, soy sauce, vinegar, broth and hot pepper sauce; set aside. Heat oil in wok over low heat. Add garlic and onion. Stir-fry until onion is soft, about 2 minutes. Increase heat to high. Add ground beef. Stir-fry until meat is no longer pink, 6 to 8 minutes. Break up meat with a wooden spoon. Stir in broth mixture, water chestnuts or sun chokes, raisins and red pepper. Stir-fry until sauce begins to thicken, 8 to 10 minutes. Stir in bean sprouts. Turn into a large serving bowl. Let each guest spoon some of hot beef mixture onto a chilled lettuce leaf. Roll up leaves jelly-roll fashion. Makes about 16 appetizer servings.

Chinese Salmon Toast

Less expensive than classic Chinese shrimp toast, but just as delicious.

1 (3-3/4-oz.) can salmon, well-drained
3/4 cup minced water chestnuts or sun chokes
1 green onion, finely chopped
1 (1-inch) cube gingerroot, minced
1 egg, slightly beaten
1 tablespoon cornstarch

1 tablespoon dry sherry
1/4 teaspoon salt
1/4 teaspoon sugar
8 or 9 thin slices firm white bread
Oil for deep frying

In a medium bowl, combine salmon, water chestnuts or sun chokes, green onion, ginger, egg, cornstarch, sherry, salt and sugar. Cut crusts from bread. Cut each slice into 4 squares. Spread 1 side of each square with salmon mixture, covering completely and mounding high. Pour oil for deep-frying into wok until 1-1/2 inches deep in center. Heat to 375F (190C). Carefully lower 6 to 8 bread squares, filling side down, into hot oil. Fry 1 minute or until sides of bread are lightly browned. Use a slotted spoon to turn squares filling side up. Fry 30 seconds or until bottom of bread is lightly browned. Lift from oil with slotted spoon. Drain on paper towels, filling side up. Fry remaining squares. Serve hot or warm. To freeze, arrange cooked squares in a single layer on a baking sheet. Place in freezer until firm. Place frozen appetizers in a plastic freezer bag or other airtight container. Store in freezer. Use within 3 weeks. To reheat frozen salmon toast, arrange in a single layer on a large baking sheet. Bake in a preheated 350F (175C) oven 20 to 25 minutes. Makes 32 to 36 appetizers.

Beef Lettuce Rolls

Greek Vegetable Stir-Fry

Add hot pita rolls and a carafe of light wine to make this a memorable midday meal.

2 tablespoons oil
2 cups cauliflowerets
1/2 lb. fresh whole green beans, trimmed
2 or 3 small zucchini, thinly sliced
1 garlic clove, crushed
1 (8-oz.) can tomato sauce
2 tablespoons Vegetable Broth, page 133,
   or water

1 teaspoon salt
1/2 teaspoon dried leaf oregano, crushed
1/4 teaspoon dried leaf rosemary, crushed
2 small tomatoes, quartered
1/2 cup pitted, black Greek olives, sliced
3 cups hot cooked rice or
   6 crisp lettuce leaves
About 1/2 cup crumbled feta cheese (2 oz.)

Heat oil in wok over high heat. Add cauliflowerets, green beans, zucchini and garlic. Stir-fry until vegetables are crisp-tender, 2 to 3 minutes. Stir in tomato sauce, broth or water, salt, oregano and rosemary. Reduce heat to low. Cover wok; simmer 5 minutes. Stir in tomatoes and olives. Spoon over rice or crisp lettuce leaves. Sprinkle each serving with 1 rounded tablespoon cheese. Makes 6 servings.

Zucchini with Pesto Sauce

Basil is usually the main ingredient in a pesto sauce, but parsley is more available.

Pesto Sauce, see below
4 medium zucchini
1 tablespoon oil

2 tablespoons water
Salt and pepper to taste
Grated Parmesan cheese

Pesto Sauce:
About 6 tablespoons olive oil
1 garlic clove, chopped
1 teaspoon salt
1/4 teaspoon pepper

1/2 cup tightly packed parsley leaves
2 tablespoons chopped walnuts
1 teaspoon dried leaf basil, crushed
2 tablespoons grated Parmesan cheese

Prepare Pesto Sauce; set aside. Cut zucchini into 2-inch slices, then into 1/4-inch-wide strips. Heat oil in wok over medium-high heat. Add zucchini strips; stir-fry 1 minute. Add water. Cover wok; simmer 2 minutes. Remove cover from wok. Stir-fry zucchini 2 minutes. Stir in Pesto Sauce and salt and pepper to taste. Spoon into a medium serving bowl. Generously sprinkle with Parmesan cheese or sprinkle Parmesan cheese on each serving. Serve hot. Makes 4 servings.

Pesto Sauce:
Combine 5 tablespoons olive oil and remaining ingredients in blender or food processor. Turning machine on and off, process until parsley and nuts are coarsely chopped. Add more oil, 1 teaspoon at a time, until sauce has consistency of heavy white sauce and is thick enough to drop from a spoon into a soft mound. To prepare by hand, place garlic and salt on a flat surface. Chop garlic until minced. Salt will absorb garlic juice. Chop parsley and nuts until minced. Combine chopped garlic, parsley, nuts, salt and remaining ingredients in a medium bowl. Beat until blended. Makes about 1 cup.

Steamed Vegetables Master Recipe

Perhaps the most flavorful of all ways to cook the good things from your garden.

About 1 lb. fresh vegetables
Salt to taste
Butter, if desired, at room temperature
Mild & Mellow Garlic Butter, page 138,
 vinaigrette dressing, Low-Calorie
 Anchovy Cream or
 Quick Curry Sauce, page 137, or
 Lemon Sauce, page 136

Rinse and trim vegetables. Place a rack in wok. Pour water into wok until 1 inch below rack. Bring water to a gentle boil over medium heat. Place vegetables on rack in a single layer or slightly over-lapping. Or arrange in a 9-inch glass pie plate. Do not crowd vegetables. If necessary, steam vegetables a few at a time, following time chart below. Adjust time as needed. Mature vegetables are tougher than young vegetables and will need slightly longer cooking times. Vegetables at room temperature will cook more quickly than chilled vegetables. Occasionally check water level in wok. If necessary, add boiling water to maintain proper level. After vegetables are cooked, remove from rack. Arrange on a platter or on serving plates. Sprinkle with salt to taste. If desired, toss hot vegetables with Mild & Mellow Garlic Butter or with vinaigrette dressing, then refriger-ate until chilled. Or serve chilled vegetables with Low-Calorie Anchovy Cream, Quick Curry Sauce or Lemon Sauce. Serve as salads or as side dishes. Makes 4 to 6 servings.

Vegetable Steaming Chart

Vegetable	Steaming Time (minutes)	Vegetable	Steaming Time (minutes)
Asparagus, medium stalks, whole	5 to 6	Mushrooms, 1/4-inch slices	5
Green beans, whole, fresh	10	Onions, 1-1/2-inch, whole;	12
frozen (10-oz.) pkg.	12	3- to 4-inch, quartered	12
Bean Sprouts	2 to 3	Peas, green, shelled	5 to 7
Beets, medium, whole	25 to 30	Peppers, bell, red or green, cut in	
Broccoli flowerets, stems 3/8-inch thick	6 to 7	1/2-inch strips	4 to 5
Brussels sprouts, medium, whole	9	Potatoes, new, red-skinned, small	15 to 20
Cabbage, green, 1-1/2 lbs., quartered	15	Potatoes, sweet or yams (6 oz. each)	25 to 30
Cabbage, green, shredded; in shallow		Snow peas, whole	4 to 5
baking dish	10	Squash, acorn, 1-1/2 lbs., cut in half	20 to 25
Cabbage, green, cut in eight wedges	11	Squash, butternut, 1-1/2 lbs., cut in half	20 to 25
Carrots, medium (4 oz. each), whole	15	Squash, zucchini or yellow summer,	
Carrots, thinly sliced	5	whole, 1-1/2 inches in diameter	8
Cauliflower, separated into flowerets	8 to 10	Squash, zucchini or yellow summer,	
Corn, freshly shucked, whole	5 to 7	1/2-inch slices	5
Eggplant, 1 lb., cut in half lengthwise	13	Turnips, white, medium (3 oz. each)	25 to 30

Vegetable Paella

A tasty blend of crisp vegetables and savory rice.

About 1/4 lb. broccoli
3 cups heavily salted cold water
2 small zucchini
1/2 medium green pepper
2 tablespoons oil
1 small onion, chopped
1 garlic clove, minced

1 (16-oz.) can tomatoes
1 teaspoon salt
1/2 teaspoon crushed dried hot red pepper
1 (7-oz.) pkg. Spanish rice mix
2-1/2 cups water
1 tablespoon butter
1 cup cooked peas

Cut broccoli in half through head and stem. Reserve half for another use. Cut flowerets from stem. Add flowerets to salty water; set aside. Chop stem into 1/2-inch dice. Cut each zucchini into 4 lengthwise strips, then into 1/2-inch pieces. Cut green pepper into 1/4-inch squares. Heat oil in wok over high heat. Add diced broccoli stems, zucchini, green pepper, onion and garlic. Stir-fry 2 to 3 minutes. Add tomatoes with juice. Use a wooden spoon to chop tomatoes. Stir in salt, red pepper, rice mix, 2-1/2 cups water and butter. Bring to a boil. Reduce heat to low. Cover wok. Simmer until most of liquid has been absorbed, about 10 minutes. Drain water from broccoli flowerets. Rinse with clear water, then pat dry with paper towels. Stir broccoli flowerets and peas into rice mixture. Cover wok; simmer 10 minutes. Remove wok from heat. Let stand, covered, 10 minutes. Fluff mixture before serving. To serve later, let stand at room temperature 2 to 3 hours in wok. Add 2 to 3 tablespoons water and reheat over low heat. Or turn paella into a 13'' x 9'' glass baking dish. Cover and refrigerate until about 35 minutes before serving. Set on counter until room temperature, about 15 minutes. Reheat 20 minutes in a 350F (175C) oven. Makes 8 servings.

How to Make Vegetable Paella

1/Trim tough end from broccoli stem. Chop broccoli stem into 1/2-inch dice.

2/Cut each zucchini into 4 lengthwise strips, then into 1/2-inch pieces.

Steamed Fresh-Vegetable Salad

A lovely addition to a party buffet table. Especially pretty arranged on a platter.

1 (2-oz.) can rolled, caper-stuffed anchovy fillets	3 medium carrots, scraped, cut in 1/2-inch slices
About 1/4 cup olive oil or vegetable oil	1/2 lb. green beans, trimmed
2 tablespoons white wine vinegar	1 medium cucumber, thinly sliced
1 tablespoon lemon juice	2 small tomatoes, cut in wedges
1 teaspoon dry mustard	Crisp lettuce leaves
1 teaspoon sugar	1/2 cup sliced, pimiento-stuffed olives
6 small new potatoes, peeled, cut in halves or quarters	

Drain anchovy fillets, reserving anchovy oil in a 1-cup measure. Set anchovies aside. Add enough olive oil or vegetable oil to anchovy oil to make 1/3 cup. Pour into a large non-metal bowl. Add vinegar, lemon juice, dry mustard and sugar. Beat with a wisk until blended. Set aside at room temperature. Place a rack in wok. Pour water into wok until 1 inch below rack. Bring to a gentle boil over medium heat. Place potatoes, carrots and beans on rack or in a 9-inch square glass baking dish. Place baking dish on rack. Cover wok. Steam 10 minutes or until vegetables are crisp-tender. Do not overcook. Add hot cooked vegetables to dressing in bowl. Toss to coat evenly. Refrigerate 1-1/2 to 2 hours until cold, or overnight. Add cucumber and tomatoes. Toss to distribute. Refrigerate until ready to serve. Line a large serving bowl or platter with lettuce leaves; set aside. Drain dressing from vegetables. Arrange vegetables on a lettuce-lined bowl or platter. Garnish with olive slices and reserved anchovy fillets. Makes 6 servings.

Spinach Salad Stir-Fry

Once you have tried this spinach salad, you'll never prepare it any other way.

1 lb. fresh spinach leaves	1 tablespoon lemon juice
6 slices thick lean bacon	1 teaspoon sugar
1 garlic clove, minced	Salt
1/2 lb. mushrooms, sliced vertically	1/2 cup croutons
1/4 cup tarragon vinegar	

Rinse spinach leaves. Pinch off stems. Pat leaves dry with paper towels; set aside. Cut bacon crosswise into 1/2-inch pieces. Stirring often, cook bacon in wok over low heat until crisp. Drain on paper towels; set aside. Reserve 1/4 cup bacon drippings in wok. Discard remaining drippings. Add garlic to reserved drippings. Stir-fry over low heat 1 minute. Increase heat to high. Add mushrooms; stir-fry 1 minute. Add trimmed spinach leaves, cooked bacon, vinegar, lemon juice and sugar. Lightly sprinkle with salt. Toss until spinach is evenly coated with dressing. Stir in croutons. Serve immediately. Makes 4 servings.

Steamed Fresh-Vegetable Salad

Eggs & Tofu

How would you like your eggs? Scrambled, fried, sunnyside up, over easy? Ho hum. What's needed are a few new ways to cook inexpensive, good-for-you eggs. The recipes in this chapter are not new, but they may be new to you. They are classic wok cookery recipes. If you liked eggs fu yung the last time you had them in a Chinese restaurant, you will undoubtedly like my puffy, little omelet cakes Monterey-style, served with chili sauce. Or perhaps you'll prefer Eggs Fu Yung with Ham & Peas in a savory sauce.

Another delightful dish that's sure to please is light and airy crepe-like omelets from Japan—Oriental Omelet Rolls. Fill them with your choice of fillings including shrimp and ham, apple and Roquefort, avocado or chicken livers. Two of the fillings are served with savory sauces and the others are topped with tangy sour cream. Good? They're delicious!

Two other recipes to give breakfast or brunch a lift are Scrambled Tofu and White-Cloud Eggs. The tofu puffs up as it scrambles and absorbs the bacon flavor from the drippings. It's a really different scramble. White-Cloud Eggs are a dieter's dream—great-tasting and calorie-affordable. Another perfect brunch dish is Ham & Eggs in Tomato Cups. They make eggs seem like a new discovery. The ham is rolled around a stuffing mixture and topped with a sauce.

Just about everyone likes tempura. Tofu, Shrimp & Vegetable Tempura, a Japanese classic, is a pleasant surprise to anyone who has never tried tofu. The tofu is marinated in a piquant sauce before it is deep-fried. The resultant flavor is delicate and tempting.◆

Celebration Brunch

Equal Amounts of Chilled Fresh Orange Juice
& Champagne
Barbecued Eggs with Mexican Crepes, page 51
Coffee
Sliced Fresh Peaches
Sprinkled with Fresh Blueberries

Scrambled Eggs with Shrimp & Ham

Light and flavorful, with just the right seasoning. Cocktail shrimp are already cleaned.

1 (6- or 8-oz.) pkg. frozen
   tiny cocktail shrimp
6 eggs
1/2 teaspoon Oriental sesame oil
1/2 teaspoon soy sauce

2 tablespoons peanut or vegetable oil
1 cup fresh bean sprouts
1 green onion, thinly sliced
1/2 cup chopped water chestnuts
1/2 cup slivered, dry-cured or smoked ham

Place unopened package of frozen shrimp in colander under cold running water, 1 minute. Turn shrimp into a colander. Set aside to finish thawing and to drain, about 5 minutes. Pat dry with paper towels; set aside. In a medium bowl, beat eggs with sesame oil and soy sauce; set aside. Heat 1 tablespoon peanut or vegetable oil in wok over medium-high heat. Add bean sprouts, green onion, water chestnuts and ham. Stir-fry 1 minute. Add thawed shrimp; stir-fry 30 seconds. Cool slightly. Stir into egg mixture. Wipe wok with paper towels. Heat remaining tablespoon peanut or vegetable oil in wok over medium heat. Pour in egg mixture. Stir-fry until eggs are softly set. Serve hot. Makes 4 servings.

Eggs Florentine

Try these for a lazy-day Sunday brunch.

1 (10-oz.) pkg. frozen spinach soufflé
4 eggs
Salt and pepper to taste
1/4 cup dairy sour cream

1/4 cup finely shredded Cheddar cheese
   (1 oz.)
Paprika

Let frozen spinach soufflé stand at room temperature until partially thawed. Remove from tray and place in a 9-inch square glass baking dish. Place a rack in wok. Pour water into wok until 1 inch below rack. Bring water to a gentle boil over medium heat. Place dish on rack. Cover wok. Steam until completely thawed, about 2 minutes. Remove dish from wok. Add boiling water to wok if needed. Bring to a gentle boil again. Spoon thawed spinach soufflé into two 10-ounce rame-kins. Spread evenly. Break 2 eggs into each ramekin. Sprinkle with salt and pepper to taste. Place filled ramekins on rack. Cover wok. Steam until eggs are set, about 8 minutes. In a small bowl, combine sour cream and cheese. Spoon evenly over cooked eggs. Sprinkle with paprika. Serve immediately. Makes 2 servings.

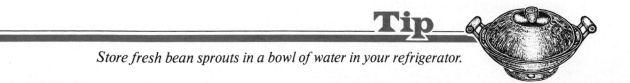

Tip

Store fresh bean sprouts in a bowl of water in your refrigerator.

Ham & Eggs in Tomato Cups

Add hot rolls and freshly brewed coffee and breakfast is served.

2 large tomatoes	4 thin slices baked ham
Salt	2 eggs
2 tablespoons butter	Salt and pepper to taste
1 small white onion, finely chopped	2 tablespoons shredded Cheddar cheese
4 large mushrooms, thinly sliced	1/2 cup dairy sour cream, room temperature
1/2 teaspoon dry mustard or	1/2 teaspoon tomato paste or ketchup
1 tablespoon Dijon-style mustard	Salt to taste
1/4 teaspoon salt	Parsley sprigs for garnish
3/4 cup herb-seasoned stuffing mix	
About 1/2 cup Chicken Broth, page 134, or	
Vegetable Broth, page 133	

Cut a thin slice from top of each tomato. Scoop out and discard seeds and pulp. Lightly sprinkle inside of tomatoes with salt. Turn cut side down on paper towels to drain. Melt butter in a small skillet. Add onion and mushrooms. Cook until tender, 2 to 3 minutes. Scrape onion, mushrooms and butter into a medium bowl. Stir in mustard, 1/4 teaspoon salt and stuffing mix. Stir in enough broth to hold mixture together. Place 1/4 of stuffing on each slice of ham. Roll up jelly-roll fashion and secure with wooden picks. Arrange in center of a 10" x 6" glass baking dish. Place 1 tomato shell in each end of dish. Carefully break 1 egg into each tomato shell. Sprinkle with salt and pepper to taste and cheese. Place a rack in wok. Pour water into wok until 1 inch below rack. Bring water to a gentle boil over medium heat. Place dish on rack. Cover wok. Steam until eggs are set, about 8 minutes. Egg whites should be firm and egg yolks set but slightly soft. In a small saucepan, combine sour cream and tomato paste or ketchup. Season with salt to taste. Stir over low heat until mixture is hot, 2 to 3 minutes. Arrange ham rolls and tomato shells on a platter. Spoon a little sour cream sauce over ham rolls. Garnish with parsley sprigs. Serve with remaining sauce. Makes 2 servings.

Scrambled Tofu

Similar to scrambled eggs, but lower in cholesterol.

2 to 4 crisp lettuce leaves	1/4 cup minced chives or green onion tops
2 slices lean bacon	2 teaspoons soy sauce
1/2 lb. tofu, crumbled	Dash pepper

Arrange lettuce leaves on 2 plates; set aside. Place bacon in cold wok over low heat. Turning occasionally, cook until crisp. Drain on paper towels. Crumble and set aside. Pour all but 1 tablespoon bacon drippings from wok. Increase heat to high. When reserved drippings are hot, add tofu. Stir-fry until fluffy, almost dry, and the consistency of soft scrambled eggs. Stir in crumbled bacon, chives or onion tops, soy sauce and pepper. Spoon tofu mixture onto lettuce leaves. Serve immediately. Makes 2 servings.

Ham & Eggs in Tomato Cups

Egg Fu Yung Monterey-Style

The eggs are prepared Chinese-style, but the sauce is definitely Mexican-style.

Monterey Sauce, see below
About 2 tablespoons oil
1/2 cup chopped walnuts
6 eggs

1/2 cup sliced pimiento-stuffed olives
1 teaspoon salt
1/2 teaspoon pepper

Monterey Sauce:
1 tablespoon oil
1 small onion, finely chopped
1/2 small green pepper, finely chopped
1 tablespoon chili powder

1 (8-oz.) can tomato sauce
1 teaspoon red wine vinegar
1/2 teaspoon sugar

Prepare Monterey Sauce; keep hot. Heat 1 tablespoon oil in wok over low heat. Add walnuts. Stir-fry until walnuts deepen in color, 1 to 2 minutes. Drain on paper towels; set aside. In a medium bowl, beat eggs until blended. Fold in toasted walnuts, olives, salt and pepper. Heat about 1 teaspoon remaining oil in wok over medium-high heat. Tip wok to distribute oil. Pour in 1/4 of egg mixture, being sure to include 1/4 of walnuts and olives. Quickly tilt wok to spread evenly. Cook until top is almost set. Do not stir. Turn with a spatula. Cook until other side is golden brown, about 30 seconds. Place cooked egg fu yung on a warm platter; keep warm. Repeat with remaining egg and oil mixture. Serve with hot Monterey Sauce. Makes 4 servings.

Monterey Sauce:
Heat oil in wok over medium-high heat. Add onion and green pepper. Stir-fry 1 minute. Stir in remaining ingredients until sauce is bubbly and hot. Makes about 1-1/4 cups.

Egg Fu Yung with Ham & Peas

A classic and elegant Chinese dish served with a quick and easy sauce.

1 (8-oz.) pkg. frozen peas with cream sauce
1/2 cup water
1 tablespoon soy sauce
3 tablespoons dry sherry
1 tablespoon cornstarch
4 eggs

1 teaspoon soy sauce
1/2 cup slivered cooked ham
2 teaspoons minced chives
1/4 cup fresh bean sprouts
4 teaspoons oil

Place frozen peas with cream sauce in top of double boiler over simmering water. Add 1/2 cup water, 1 tablespoon soy sauce and 1 tablespoon sherry. When peas and sauce are thawed, stir to blend; keep hot. In a medium bowl, stir remaining 2 tablespoons sherry into cornstarch. Add eggs. Beat until blended. Fold in 1 teaspoon soy sauce, ham, chives and bean sprouts. Heat 1 teaspoon oil in wok over medium-high heat. Tip wok to distribute oil. Pour in about 1/4 of egg mixture, being sure to include 1/4 of ham, chives and bean sprouts. Quickly tilt wok to spread evenly. Cook 30 seconds or until almost set. Turn with a spatula. Cook other side until lightly browned, about 30 seconds. Place on a warm platter; keep warm. Repeat with remaining oil and egg mixture. Arrange 2 egg fu yung on each of 2 plates, slightly overlapping. Spoon hot peas and sauce over each serving. Serve immediately. Makes 2 servings.

Rice, Pasta & Bulgar

Most people don't fully appreciate the versatility of rice, pasta and bulgar. They usually serve them unadorned and only as an accompaniment to meat. What a waste! Any of them can be sauced and seasoned in literally hundreds of ways to make them the main course and star attraction of the meal.

At the beginning of this chapter are some basic recipes, but I've also given you a sampling of recipes for inspired rice, pasta and bulgar cookery. You'll find many more ways to use these multi-purpose foods throughout this book.

Cook-Ahead Rice gives you complete instructions for cooking rice, refrigerating it and reheating it. You'll be delighted to learn you can reheat cold cooked rice and have it just as light, fluffy and delicious as when it was freshly cooked. The secret is in the steaming.

Bulgar, most popular in mid-Eastern countries, is also becoming a favorite of many other countries. Bulgar is made by cooking whole-kernel wheat until the kernels become tender and begin to burst. It is then dried and cracked. Add a handful of bulgar to stews or soups for stick-to-the-ribs goodness and full-bodied flavor. It cooks by the time it absorbs moisture. Bulgar Pilaf is a delicious combination of bulgar, raisins, onions, pine nuts and spices cooked in broth. Serve it as a main dish or as a substitute for rice or potatoes. ❖

Dinner for Special Guests

Fruits de Mer au Riz, page 69
Icy-Cold Spirited Drinks
Mediterranean Chicken, page 127
Hot Cook-Ahead Rice, page 63
Beaujolais or other Light Red Wine
Pink-Cloud Meringue Cake, page 142
Coffee with Brandy

Thin Noodles or Other Fine Pasta

Use this method to cook thin spaghetti or fine noodles.

4 qts. water
1 tablespoon oil
1 tablespoon salt

1 lb. fine noodles or other fine pasta
2 tablespoons butter or 1 tablespoon oil

In a 6-quart pot, bring water to a rolling boil over high heat. Add 1 tablespoon oil and salt. Add noodles or other pasta, a few at a time, so water continues to boil. Stirring once, boil uncovered 2 minutes. Remove pot from heat. Cover first with a clean cloth then with lid. Let stand 8 or 9 minutes, but no longer. Pour into a colander to drain. Turn drained pasta into a medium serving bowl. Toss with butter or 1 tablespoon oil. Makes 6 to 8 servings.

Fresh Chinese Noodles

Use these noodles as a substitute for other noodles.

4 cups water
1/2 lb. fresh Chinese noodles

1-1/2 cups cold water

In a large saucepan, bring 4 cups water to a rolling boil over high heat. Slowly add noodles, stirring gently with a fork to separate. Bring water back to a rolling boil. Add 1-1/2 cups cold water. Again bring water to a rolling boil. Immediately pour noodle mixture into a colander to drain. Turn drained noodles into a medium serving bowl. Makes 4 servings.

Stir-Fried Rice with Pork

A hearty supper from that last bit of roast pork.

1 tablespoon oil
1 small green pepper, finely chopped
1 small white onion, finely chopped
1/2 lb. cooked lean pork, coarsely chopped

3 cups cold cooked rice
2 tablespoons soy sauce
2 eggs, slightly beaten
1 green onion, minced

Heat oil in wok. Add green pepper and white onion. Stir-fry 1 minute. Add pork, rice and soy sauce. Stir-fry 3 minutes or until hot. Pour eggs over pork mixture. Stir-fry 1 to 2 minutes or until eggs are set. Sprinkle each serving with minced green onion. Makes 4 servings.

Variation

Substitute cooked lamb or beef for cooked pork.

Clockwise from top: Golden Rice, page 62, Stir-Fried Rice with Vegetables, page 62, Bulgar Pilaf, page 66.

Bulgar Pilaf   Photo on page 61.

A superb alternative to rice or potatoes.

2-1/2 cups Chicken Broth, page 134, or Vegetable Broth, page 133	1 tablespoon butter 1/2 cup raisins
1 tablespoon oil	1/2 cup toasted pine nuts
2 or 3 green onions, thinly sliced	1/2 teaspoon salt
2/3 cup bulgar	1/4 teaspoon white pepper

In a small saucepan, bring broth to a boil over medium heat; keep hot. Heat oil in wok over medium-high heat. Add green onions; stir-fry 1 minute. Add bulgar; stir-fry 30 seconds. Stir in hot broth, butter, raisins, pine nuts, salt and white pepper. Bring to a boil. Immediately reduce heat to medium. Cover wok; simmer 20 minutes or until liquid is absorbed. Makes 6 servings.

Armenian Noodles & Rice

Another way to make rice special!

1/4 cup butter	1 teaspoon turmeric
1/4 lb. small egg noodles	1 teaspoon salt
1 cup long-grain rice, uncooked	3 cups hot water

Melt butter in wok over medium heat. Break noodles into 1-inch pieces. Cook and stir noodles in melted butter, 5 minutes. Add rice, turmeric and salt. Add hot water. Stir while bringing to a boil. Reduce heat to medium-low. Cover wok. Simmer 15 minutes or until rice is tender but not mushy. Drain and turn into a medium bowl. Let stand 1 minute. Fluff with 2 forks. Serve immediately or return rice mixture to colander. Place colander over a pan of simmering water. Lay wet paper towels directly on rice mixture until ready to serve. Makes 4 servings.

Saffron Rice

The ultimate luxury in rice cookery.

1/2 cup currants	1/2 teaspoon salt
1/2 cup water	3 or 4 drops oil
1/2 teaspoon saffron threads	1 tablespoon butter
2 tablespoons lemon juice	1 cup long-grain rice, uncooked
4 cups water	

In a small saucepan, combine currants, 1/2 cup water, saffron and lemon juice. Stir over low heat 3 to 5 minutes or until water is reduced to 2 tablespoons and saffron has dissolved; set aside. Pour 4 cups water into wok. Bring to a rolling boil. Add salt, oil and butter. Slowly stir in rice, being sure water continues to boil. Boil 15 to 17 minutes until rice is tender but not mushy. Pour into a colander to drain. Turn rice mixture into a medium serving bowl. Add plumped-currant mixture. Gently toss with 2 forks. Serve immediately or return rice to colander. Place colander over a pan of simmering water. Lay wet paper towels directly on rice until ready to serve. Makes 4 servings.

French-Fried Butte

So easy to prepare in your wok.

1-1/2 lbs. fresh shrimp
1 egg, separated
Oil for deep frying
3/4 cup all-purpose flour
1/4 cup cornstarch

Shell shrimp, leaving shell on tails. Rem
way through back. Rinse shrimp under r
small bowl, beat egg white until soft pea
Pour oil for deep-frying into wok until 1
While oil heats, combine flour, cornstar
blespoons oil and beaten egg yolk. Beat u
batter. Turning once, fry 2 or 3 shrimp at
Drain on paper towels. Serve hot with Rén

Fruits de Mer au R

This steamed seafood over Saffron Rice, page

4 to 6 clams in shells
Cold water
2 tablespoons cornmeal
4 to 6 jumbo shrimp in shells
2 sole fillets or flounder fillets

Place clams in a large pot. Pour in cold
Drain. Use a soft brush to scrub clams un
ing easy. Shell shrimp, leaving shell on tai
clams, shrimp and fish aside. Place a racl
Bring to a gentle boil over medium heat.
9-inch round baking dish. Arrange toma
Place dish on rack. Cover wok; steam 5
strips and scallops over rice. Cover wok.
fish strips and scallops are firm, 3 to 4 m
with soy sauce. Serve from dish. Makes 2

Use a slotted spoon to lift cooke

Fish & Seafood

All foods take less time to cook in a wok, especially fish. If you cook fish longer than the time recommended in the following recipes, you will rob the fish of its delicious juices, making it dry. Never cook fish until it flakes.

In this chapter are some superb recipes *written in steam.* Steaming is a method of cooking that is ideally suited to almost all fish and shellfish. Once you have tasted steamed fish, you may never again poach or bake it. See page 8 for other information on steaming.

You'll find fresh and frozen ingredients used interchangeably in these recipes. The reason is simple. Nothing is quite as delicious as fish fresh from a stream, lake or ocean and immediately cooked. It's not always possible to indulge in this luxury. What is possible, however, is to cook frozen fish as soon as it is thawed. In my opinion, freshly thawed fish tastes fresher than supposedly fresh fish that may actually be several days old.

Most frozen fish is processed on ships the day it is caught.

If you are looking for a dish for entertaining, Tempura Fish Strips & Zucchini is especially nice. It not only tastes good, but doesn't have to be served portion-by-portion as it is cooked. The food can wait until all portions are cooked before being served.❖

Dinner with Good Friends

Western Won Tons, page 22
Assorted Fillings, pages 22 and 23
Tempura Fish Strips & Zucchini, page 78
Cold Beer
Preserved Kumquats
Candied Ginger
Fresh Grapes
Coffee

Chutney Shrimp

Incredibly easy. Exceptionally good.

2 (8-oz.) pkgs. frozen tiny shrimp
2 tablespoons cornstarch
1/2 cup dry sherry
1/4 cup butter
2-1/2 teaspoons curry powder or to

Place unopened packages of frozen
into a colander. Set aside to finish
sherry; set aside. Melt butter in wo
in sherry mixture, chutney and shell
medium serving bowl. Spoon chutn
ing with 2 tablespoons peanuts, 1
servings.

Jade-Tree Shrim

The name tells you this dish looks as gr

4 to 6 cups water
1/4 cup salt
About 1 lb. broccoli
1 tablespoon oil
1 garlic clove, crushed
1 (1-inch) cube gingerroot, crushed

Pour water into a large saucepan. S
flowerets in salted water. Let stand
stems. Cut remaining stems crossw
aside. Heat oil in wok over low
browned. Discard garlic and ginger.
stem strips. Stir-fry 1 minute. Ad
minute. Add broccoli flowerets. Si
pink, about 1 minute. Stir in soy sau

Tip

Never use corn oil to s

Tom Lee's Szechuan Shrimp

A great Chinese-American chef adapted this recipe especially for this book.

1 lb. fresh or frozen medium to large
   shrimp, thawed
1/2 cup thinly sliced green onions
1/2 cup minced bamboo shoots
1 (1-inch) cube gingerroot, minced
1 garlic clove, minced
1/2 cup ketchup

1/4 cup dry sherry
1 tablespoon soy sauce
1 teaspoon sugar
1 teaspoon Oriental sesame oil
1/2 teaspoon crushed dried hot red pepper
1 tablespoon peanut or vegetable oil
3 cups hot cooked Chinese egg noodles or rice

Shell shrimp; remove veins. Set cleaned shrimp aside. In a small bowl, combine green onions, bamboo shoots, ginger and garlic. In another small bowl, combine ketchup, sherry, soy sauce, sugar, sesame oil and red pepper. Heat peanut or vegetable oil in wok over high heat. Add green onion mixture; stir-fry 1 minute. Add shrimp; stir-fry 2 minutes. Stir in ketchup mixture until hot. Serve over Chinese egg noodles or rice. Makes 4 servings.

Pink Shrimp & Green Peas

Keep frozen shrimp and peas on hand in your freezer for this festive dish.

1 (8-oz.) pkg. frozen tiny shrimp
1 tablespoon cornstarch
2 tablespoons dry sherry
2 tablespoons soy sauce
1 teaspoon Oriental sesame oil, if desired
Oil for deep-frying

2 cups hot cooked rice
1 (10-oz.) pkg. frozen tiny peas,
   thawed, drained
1/2 cup Chicken Broth, page 134, or
   Vegetable Broth, page 133

Place unopened package of frozen shrimp under cold running water, 1 minute. Turn shrimp into a colander to drain and finish thawing. In a medium non-metal bowl, stir cornstarch into sherry. Stir in soy sauce and sesame oil, if desired. Add shrimp. Set aside to marinate 15 minutes. Pour oil for deep-frying into wok until 1-1/2 inches deep in center. Heat to 350F (175C). Place rice in a large serving bowl. Set aside and keep hot. Place peas in a large metal sieve. Lower sieve into hot oil. Cook peas 1 minute. Hold sieve over wok to drain. Spoon cooked peas over hot rice. Drain marinated shrimp, reserving marinade in a small saucepan. Place drained marinated shrimp in metal sieve. Lower sieve into hot oil. Cook shrimp 30 seconds. Hold sieve over wok to drain. Spoon cooked shrimp over peas; keep warm. Pour broth into reserved marinade. Stir over medium heat until thickened. Spoon over cooked shrimp and peas. Makes 2 servings.

Tom Lee's Szechuan Shrimp with Green Beans & Mushrooms, page 37

Crisp Trout Malaysian-Style

Delicately steamed fish with crisp onions and a flavorful sauce.

1 (2- to 2-1/2-lb.) trout or
  other white fish
3 tablespoons dry sherry
2 tablespoons soy sauce
1 canned hot green pepper

1 large mild red onion
2 tablespoons oil
1/4 cup soy sauce
3 cups hot cooked rice or Saffron Rice,
  page 66

Cut 4 or 5 diagonal slashes on both sides of fish. Place in a shallow 2-quart round or oval baking dish. In a small bowl, combine sherry and 2 tablespoons soy sauce. Pour over fish. Turn fish to cover both sides with sauce. Place a rack in wok. Pour water into wok until 1 inch below rack. Bring to a gentle boil over medium heat. Place dish on rack. Cover wok. Steam 20 to 25 minutes until fish is opaque. Weight of fish will affect cooking time. While fish cooks, drain hot pepper on paper towels. Remove and discard seeds. Finely chop hot pepper; set aside. Slice onion vertically into 1/4-inch slices. Separate slices into strips; set aside. When fish has 2 to 3 minutes cooking time left, heat oil in a medium skillet. Add onion strips. Stir-fry over high heat until very crisp and browned, about 4 minutes. Do not burn. Stir in chopped hot pepper. Add 1/4 cup soy sauce all at once. When spattering stops, pour onion mixture over fish. Serve with hot cooked rice or Saffron Rice. Or serve as part of an Oriental buffet. Makes 2 to 4 servings.

Scallop Chop Suey

If you're a seafood lover, you'll love this dish.

2 tablespoons oil
1 lb. large fresh scallops, sliced
1 small onion, chopped
1 green pepper, chopped
1 (16-oz.) pkg. frozen Chinese-style
  vegetables, thawed
1/2 cup fresh bean sprouts

1/4 cup water
1 tablespoon oyster sauce
1/4 cup water
1 teaspoon cornstarch
2 to 3 cups hot Golden Rice, page 62
1/2 cup Chinese fried noodles

Heat 1 tablespoon oil in wok over high heat. Add scallops. Stir-fry until opaque, about 3 minutes. Drain on paper towels. Heat remaining tablespoon oil in wok. Add onion and green pepper. Stir-fry 1 minute. Add Chinese-style vegetables, bean sprouts and 1/4 cup water. Stir in oyster sauce. Stir-fry 2 minutes. Cover wok. Simmer until vegetables are crisp-tender, about 3 minutes. In a small bowl, stir 1/4 cup water into cornstarch. Stir into vegetable mixture. Add cooked scallops. Gently stir until heated through, about 2 minutes. Spoon over Golden Rice. Sprinkle each serving with some of Chinese fried noodles. Makes 4 servings.

 **Tip**

After frying in your wok, wash it in hot soapy water. Dry it immediately.

Salmon

An especially lovel

1 (8-oz.) can sal
2 tablespoons m
1/2 teaspoon dri
1/2 teaspoon pa
2 tablespoons l
1 head Boston l

Lemon Sauce:
3 tablespoons
2 tablespoons
1 cup boiling
1/4 cup lemor

Turn salmon
Remove 4 br
off coarse rit
at a time, un
each leaf. Fo
Place a rack
medium he
on opposite
dish. Add t
Sauce. Arra
over and an

Lemon Sa
In a medi
boiling wa
in yogurt

Salm

Fresh gir

1 (8-oz.
2 tables
2 cups
1 green
1/4 cup

Drain
8-inch
rice, §
salmo
over
salmo

Sweet & Sour Fish

Tender, crisp strips of fish with just the right piquant sauce.

1/4 cup slivered candied ginger	1 cup Chicken Broth, page 134, or
1/4 cup dry sherry	Vegetable Broth, page 133
2 tablespoons cornstarch	2 tablespoons dry sherry
1-1/2 lbs. fish fillets,	1/4 cup saké or white wine vinegar
cut in 1/2-inch strips	1 tablespoon oil
Oil for deep-frying	1 small green pepper, cut in
3 tablespoons soy sauce	1/2-inch squares
1/3 cup packed brown sugar	1 small onion, chopped
2 tablespoons cornstarch	

Rinse excess sugar from ginger. Place rinsed ginger in a small bowl. Sprinkle with 1/4 cup sherry; set aside. Spoon 2 tablespoons cornstarch into a pie plate. Roll fish strips in cornstarch to coat on all sides. Pour oil for deep-frying into wok until 1-1/2 inches deep in center. Heat oil to 350F (175C). Fry fish strips, a few at a time, in hot oil until golden brown, 3 to 4 minutes. Drain on paper towels; set aside. In a small bowl, combine soy sauce, brown sugar, 2 tablespoons cornstarch, broth, 2 tablespoons sherry and saké or vinegar; set aside. Pour used oil from wok. Wipe wok with paper towels. Heat 1 tablespoon oil in wok over high heat. Add green pepper and onion. Stir-fry 30 seconds. Add soy sauce mixture and ginger mixture. Stir over high heat until sauce thickens, about 1 minute. Arrange cooked fish on a medium platter. Pour sauce over fish. Serve immediately. Makes 4 servings.

Sole with Sesame Sauce

Serve this beautiful combination in the dish it was steamed in.

1 small lemon	1-1/2 cups cold Saffron Rice, page 66,
2 cups boiling water	Golden Rice, page 62, or
2 medium sole fillets	cooked white rice
2 teaspoons Oriental sesame oil	1/4 cup slivered almonds
2 teaspoons soy sauce	1-1/2 cups cold cooked peas
1 teaspoon white wine vinegar	
2 green onions, cut in	
2-inch julienne strips	

Slice off both ends of lemon. Reserve ends for another use. Cut remaining lemon into thin slices. Cut slices in half. In a medium bowl, pour boiling water over lemon slices. Let stand 15 minutes. Drain; set lemon slices aside. Place fish on a flat surface, skin side down. Fold ends of each fillet toward center to make a 3- to 4-inch square. Place fish squares side-by-side in center of a 10'' x 6'' baking dish. In a small bowl, combine sesame oil, soy sauce and vinegar. Pour over fish. Sprinkle onion strips over fish. In a medium bowl, combine rice and almonds. Alternately spoon mounds of rice mixture and green peas into dish around fish. Separate each mound with a halved lemon slice, curved side up. Place a rack in wok. Pour water into wok until 1 inch below rack. Bring to a gentle boil over medium heat. Place dish on rack. Cover wok. Steam 10 minutes or until fish is opaque and rice and peas are hot. Makes 2 servings.

__ How to

1/Holding core
boiling water ur

Fillet of Sole Florentine

Tantalizing, steamed-in flavor and no work make this the perfect lazy-night supper dish.

1 small tomato, cut in narrow wedges
1 cup packed fresh spinach leaves, rinsed,
   blotted dry
2 tablespoons lemon juice

2 tablespoons soy sauce
1 sole fillet, cut in half crosswise
8 Enoki mushrooms, if desired

Remove and discard tomato seeds and pulp; set aside. Cut two 12-inch squares of foil. Lightly oil half of each square. Place half of spinach on each oiled portion. Combine lemon juice and soy sauce. Sprinkle half of lemon juice mixture over spinach. Top each with 1 piece of fish. Sprinkle fish with remaining lemon juice mixture. Top each with half of tomato strips and half of mushrooms, if desired. Working with 1 piece of foil at a time, loosely fold unoiled portion over top of stacked ingredients, bringing edges together. Leave an air space over contents. Fold edges together, making 2 or 3 turns. Fold up both ends of foil, making an airtight package. Or fold as in photos. Steam immediately or refrigerate up to 1 hour. To steam, place a rack in wok. Pour water into wok until 1 inch below rack. Bring to a gentle boil over medium heat. Arrange packets on rack. Cover wok; steam 6 minutes. To serve, cut a large X in top of each packet. Fold back foil. Arrange packets on a platter or on individual plates. Makes 2 servings.

__ How to Make Fillet of Sole Florentine __

1/Layer half of spinach, fish, tomatoes and mushrooms on
each piece of foil. Sprinkle with lemon-juice mixture.

2/Leave an air space over contents. Fold foil edges together. Fold up ends of foil, making an airtight package.

Tu

A

1/
1
1/
2
1

I
b
8

Steamed Shrimp

Serve these tender, juicy shrimp with Rémoulade Sauce or Sauce Romanoff, page 135.

Shrimp size	Number of shrimp per lb.	Steaming time for 1 lb. shrimp
Jumbo shrimp	12 to 14	3 minutes
Large shrimp	16 to 24	2-1/2 minutes
Medium shrimp	23 to 25	2 minutes

Place a rack in wok. Pour water into wok until 1 inch below rack. Bring to a gentle boil over medium heat. Shell shrimp, leaving shell on tails. Use a small, sharp knife to remove veins. Arrange shelled shrimp in a single layer or slightly overlapping on rack. Or arrange shrimp in a shallow 9-inch square baking dish. Place dish on rack. Cover wok. Steam according to time above. Makes 2 to 3 servings.

Steamed Lobster

The ultimate luxury in seafood.

2 (1- to 2-lb.) live lobsters
Lemon-Butter Dip, page 138, Lemony Mayonnaise, page 139, or Tartar Sauce, page 137.

Lobster size	Steaming time	Standing time
1 lb.	3 minutes	10 minutes
1-1/4 to 1-1/2 lbs.	4 to 5 minutes	10 minutes
1-1/2 to 2 lbs.	5 to 6 minutes	10 minutes

Keep lobster alive and on ice until ready to steam. Place rack in wok. Pour water into wok until 1 inch below rack. Bring to a rolling boil over high heat. Place live lobsters on rack. Cover wok. Steam according to time above. Remove wok from heat. Let stand, covered, for standing time. Remove lobsters from wok. When cool enough to handle, turn each lobster on its back. With a sharp, heavy knife split each lobster down the middle and remove stomach and intestinal vein. They are easily identifiable in the tail section close to the back shell. Leave liver and roe in the shell. They are superb eating. Serve warm with Lemon-Butter Dip or refrigerate until chilled and serve with Lemony Mayonnaise or Tartar Sauce. Makes 2 servings.

Tip

Use your imagination when combining foods for stir-frying. Just before serving, add those that need little time to cook.

Tempura Fish Strips & Zucchini

The cook's favorite tempura because it is so easy to make and use.

2 medium zucchini
Oil for deep-frying
1/2 cup all-purpose flour
1 tablespoon cornstarch
1 teaspoon baking powder
1 egg white
About 1/4 cup cold club soda
1 lb. fish fillets, cut in 1/2-inch strips

3 tablespoons soy sauce
1/2 cup Dashi, page 133, or
    Vegetable Broth, page 133
2 tablespoons mirin wine or
    2 tablespoons dry sherry plus
    1 tablespoon sugar
4 cups hot cooked rice

Cut zucchini crosswise into 1-inch pieces. Cut each piece lengthwise into thin slices; set aside. Pour oil for deep-frying into wok until 1-1/2 inches deep in center. Heat oil to 350F (175C). Preheat oven to 200F (95C). While oil heats, sift flour, cornstarch and baking powder into a medium bowl. Stir in egg white then club soda, 1 tablespoon at a time, until batter has consistency of heavy cream. Dip fish strips into batter. Drain slightly over bowl. Use tongs to lower batter-coated fish strips into hot oil. Turning once, fry 3 or 4 at a time until lightly browned, about 30 seconds. Drain on paper towels. Arrange in one end of a 10" x 6" baking dish. Place in preheated oven to keep warm. Dip zucchini slices into batter. Fry 2 or 3 at a time until golden brown and crisp, 30 to 60 seconds. Drain on paper towels. Place in dish with fish. Combine soy sauce, Dashi or broth and mirin or sherry and sugar in a small saucepan. Stir over medium-high heat until slightly reduced, 1 to 2 minutes. To serve, divide rice among 4 small deep bowls. Spoon about 2 tablespoons soy-sauce mixture over rice in each bowl. Divide fish and zucchini strips equally among bowls. Sprinkle evenly with remaining soy-sauce mixture. Makes 4 servings.

Creole Fish Fillets

Frozen fish fillets are transformed into New Orleans-style haute cuisine.

1 lb. frozen fish fillets, partially thawed
1 egg white
1/2 cup cornstarch
4 to 5 tablespoons oil
1 small green pepper, cut in
    1/2-inch squares
1 small onion, finely chopped
2 medium tomatoes, chopped

2 tablespoons chili sauce
1 teaspoon sugar
2 to 3 drops hot pepper sauce
2 teaspoons lemon juice
1/4 cup clam juice
1 teaspoon salt
3 cups hot cooked rice or Golden Rice,
    page 62

Cut partially thawed fish fillets into 2" x 1" strips. Place egg white in a medium bowl. Pour cornstarch into a pie plate. Dip fish strips in egg white, then cornstarch. Heat 3 to 4 tablespoons oil in wok over high heat. Add coated fish pieces, a few at a time. Fry 1 minute. Turn carefully to keep from crumbling. Fry 30 seconds longer. Drain on paper towels. Set aside and keep warm. Add remaining tablespoon oil to hot wok. Add green pepper and onion. Stir-fry 2 minutes. Add tomatoes; stir-fry 1 minute. Cover wok; simmer 30 seconds. Stir in chili sauce, sugar, hot pepper sauce, lemon juice, clam juice and salt. Carefully stir in cooked fish. Heat 1 minute. Serve over hot cooked rice or Golden Rice. Makes 4 servings.

Chicken & Turkey

hicken is choice, versatile and inexpensive. As good cooks everywhere know, no other meat adapts so well to so many different ways of cooking. It can be stir-fried, deep-fried, steamed or seared in a wok. Cook it with vegetables, fruit, cashews or almonds. Literally hundreds of spices and sauces can be used to complement and bring out its delectable flavor.

Wok-cooked chicken has exceptional flavor and is nutritious. What more could you ask, except that it be quick and easy to prepare? The recipes here, like all wok cookery, are just that. Not one takes more than an hour from start to table. Most are even quicker.

Any good chicken dish starts at the market. The ideal chicken for wok cooking is a 2-1/2- to 3-1/2-pound broiler-fryer. It should be plump and unblemished and have a fresh aroma. Skin color can be any shade from pure white to golden yellow, depending on how the bird was fed. Color doesn't affect flavor. Look for chicken with thin, tightly fitting, moist-looking skin, without fatty deposits. The breast bone should be flexible and covered with a thick layer of meat.

Unwrap chicken as soon as you get home from the market. Remove the giblets and liver from the cavity and wrap the chicken loosely to let air circulate around it. Store it in the coolest part of your refrigerator for no more than two days. Wrap airtight and freeze any chicken you don't plan to use within a short time. It can be stored in the freezer up to 3 months. Defrost poultry in the refrigerator or in cold water while still wrapped. Never defrost poultry at room temperature. Harmful bacteria grow rapidly at room temperature. ❖

Big Family Get-Together Party

Nabe Mono Delight, page 26
Chinese Chicken with Vegetables, page 97
Noodles
Lemon Angel, page 145
Coffee

Turkey Cutlets à la Holstein

Picture-pretty: Tender turkey cutlets and beans garnished with apricots, lemons and cream.

4 turkey cutlets
1/2 cup all-purpose flour
1 teaspoon salt
1/8 teaspoon pepper
1 cup fine dry breadcrumbs
2 eggs
1 tablespoon water
Oil for deep-frying
1 tablespoon oil

1 cup diagonally sliced celery
1 (10-oz.) pkg. frozen baby lima beans
1 teaspoon garlic powder
1/2 teaspoon salt
1 (8-oz.) can apricot halves
3/4 cup Vegetable Broth, page 133,
    Chicken Broth, page 134, or water
About 2 tablespoons sour cream for garnish
Lemon wedges for garnish

Place each turkey cutlet between 2 sheets of waxed paper. With a rolling pin or side of heavy cleaver, pound turkey cutlets until 1/4 inch thick. Cut each flattened cutlet in half; set aside. Combine flour, salt and pepper in a pie plate. Spread breadcrumbs in another pie plate. In a small shallow bowl, beat eggs and 1 tablespoon water. Roll cutlet halves in flour mixture. Dip in egg mixture, then coat with crumbs. Pour oil for deep-frying into wok until 1-1/2 inches deep in center. Heat oil to 350F (175C). Turning once, fry coated cutlets in hot oil until golden brown, 2 to 3 minutes. Drain on paper towels; keep warm. Pour oil from wok. Wipe wok with paper towels. Heat 1 tablespoon oil in wok over medium-high heat. Add celery; stir-fry 1 minute. Add beans, garlic powder and 1/2 teaspoon salt. Drain apricots, reserving juice. Add reserved juice and broth or water to celery mixture. Bring to a boil. Reduce heat to low. Cover wok. Simmer 15 minutes or until beans are tender and most of liquid has evaporated. Spoon onto center of a large platter. Arrange cooked turkey cutlets around celery mixture. Top each cutlet with an apricot half. Garnish with sour cream and lemon wedges. Makes 4 servings.

Turkey & Pork Zurich-Style

A Swiss classic for your wok.

2 tablespoons oil
1/2 lb. large mushrooms, thinly sliced
1/2 lb. boneless lean pork,
  cut in thin slices
1/2 cup dry sherry
1/2 lb. turkey cutlets,
  cut in very thin slices

1/4 cup Chicken Broth, page 134, or
    Vegetable Broth, page 133
1 cup dairy sour cream
1 tablespoon finely minced chives
1 tablespoon finely minced parsley
Salt and pepper to taste
Fine noodles, cooked, drained

Heat 1 tablespoon oil in wok over high heat. Add mushrooms; stir-fry 1 minute. Spoon into a medium bowl; set aside. Heat remaining tablespoon oil in wok over high heat. Add pork slices; stir-fry 1 minute. Add sherry. Cover wok; simmer 3 minutes. Add turkey slices. Cook until firm, about 1 minute. Add cooked mushrooms and broth. Cover wok. Simmer until most of liquid has evaporated, about 5 minutes. Remove wok from heat. Gently stir in sour cream, chives, parsley and salt and pepper to taste. Place wok over low heat. Stir until mixture is hot but not boiling, 30 seconds. Serve over noodles. Makes 4 servings.

Cornish Hens Peking-Style

Game hens are steamed, then deep-fried in this adaptation of a classic Chinese dish.

2 frozen Rock Cornish game hens, thawed
1/4 cup boiling water
1/2 cup packed brown sugar
1 tablespoon dry mustard

1/2 cup dry sherry
1/4 cup soy sauce
Oil for deep-frying

Remove gizzard, liver and neck from each hen. Reserve for soup or broth. Rinse hens inside and out under cold running water. With a sharp knife or poultry shears, cut each hen in half lengthwise; set aside. Place a rack in wok. Pour water into wok until 1 inch below rack. Bring water to a gentle boil over medium heat. Arrange halved hens on rack. Cover wok; steam 25 minutes. Arrange steamed hens in a single layer in two 9-inch square glass baking dishes. Pour water from wok. Wipe wok dry with paper towels. In a small bowl, pour 1/4 cup boiling water over sugar and mustard. Stir until dissolved. Stir in sherry and soy sauce. Pour over steamed hens. Marinate 1 hour, turning and basting often. Pour oil for deep-frying into wok until 1-1/2 inches deep in center. Heat oil to 350F (175C). Fry each hen half until browned and crisp, 5 to 7 minutes on each side. Add more oil, if necessary. Serve hot or at room temperature. Makes 2 to 4 servings.

Cornish Hens with Fruited Stuffing

Tender, juicy birds with crispy, brown skin.

2 frozen Rock Cornish game hens, thawed
2 tablespoons rice wine or brandy
1 teaspoon salt
3 tablespoons butter
1 small onion, minced
1 cup packaged herb stuffing mix
1/4 cup frozen orange juice concentrate, thawed

1 small apple, peeled, cored, minced
1/4 cup raisins
1/2 cup coarsely chopped pecans
2 eggs
1 teaspoon soy sauce
1/2 cup all-purpose flour
1/4 cup water

Remove liver and gizzards from hens; set aside. Rinse hens inside and out under cold running water. Pat dry with paper towels. Rub each hen with wine or brandy and salt. Let stand at room temperature 15 minutes. Coarsely chop liver and gizzards. Melt 2 tablespoons butter in a small saucepan over medium heat. Add chopped liver and gizzards. Cook and stir until browned, 2 to 3 minutes. Spoon into a medium bowl; set aside. Melt remaining tablespoon butter in pan. Add onion. Cook and stir until soft, about 1 minute. Spoon into cooked liver mixture. Stir in stuffing mix, orange juice concentrate, apple, raisins and pecans. In a small bowl, lightly beat 1 egg. Stir into dressing mixture. Stuff each bird with half of mixture. Tuck wing tips under back of hen. Tie legs together with string. Pull loose neck skin over and into neck opening. Place a rack in wok. Pour water into wok until 1 inch below rack. Bring water to a gentle boil over medium heat. Place stuffed hens on rack, breast up. Cover wok; steam 30 minutes. Preheat oven to 375F (190C). Beat remaining egg in a small bowl. Stir in soy sauce, flour and water until smooth. Brush egg mixture over entire surface of each hen. Bake 15 minutes or until a deep, golden brown. Makes 2 to 4 servings.

Cornish Hens Peking-Style with Orange Rice Ring, page 65

Chicken with Teri[...]

Nobody, but nobody, can resist this scrumptio[...]

12 chicken thighs, skinned, boned
1/2 cup teriyaki sauce
1/2 cup dry sherry
1 (1-inch) cube gingerroot, shredded, or
   1 teaspoon ground ginger
1 garlic clove, minced
1 teaspoon sugar

Cut chicken into 3/4-inch pieces. Set aside[...]
sor, combine teriyaki sauce, sherry, ginge[...]
pureed. Pour over chicken pieces. Let stand[...]
marinade. Combine 1/4 cup cornstarch and[...]
ture. Shake off excess. Heat oil in wok over[...]
pieces in hot oil, a few at a time, until crisp[...]
towels. Pour oil from wok. Wipe with paper[...]
gentle boil over medium heat. In a small bo[...]
into hot marinade until sauce is thickened, 1[...]
hot, 30 seconds. Serve with rice. Makes 4 ser[...]

Chicken Sambal

Sambal is a mixture of Maylasian or Indonesian c[...]

1/2 small lemon
4 chicken breast halves, skinned, boned
2 tablespoons oil
1 medium onion, chopped
1 garlic clove, minced
1/4 lb. mushrooms, thinly sliced

Cut peel from lemon in a thin layer, being caref[...]
strips. Squeeze juice from lemon. Set peel and[...]
strips. Heat 1 tablespoon oil in wok over high[...]
white, 6 to 8 minutes. Drain on paper towels.[...]
heat. Add onion, garlic and mushrooms. Stir-fr[...]
tomatoes with juice. Use a wooden spoon to bre[...]
heat until mixture just simmers. Add soy sauc[...]
cooked chicken strips until coated with sauce. C[...]
Garnish each serving with a sprinkling of green on[...]

Mandarin Chick

Oriental marinade flavors and glazes t

4 chicken breast halves, skinned, b
1/4 cup honey
3/4 cup boiling water
1 garlic clove, crushed
1 (1-inch) cube gingerroot, crushed
1/3 cup cornstarch
Oil for deep-frying
1 tablespoon oil
1/4 lb. mushrooms, sliced

Cut chicken crosswise into 1/2-inch st
water. Stir in chicken strips, garlic and
spoon to lift chicken from marinade.
cornstarch; set aside. Remove and disc
frying into wok until 1-1/2 inches dee
strips, a few at a time, in hot oil unti
Pour oil from wok. Wipe wok with pa
Add mushrooms; stir-fry 1 to 2 minut
Reduce heat to medium. Cover wok; si
In a small bowl, combine 1 tablespoon
until liquid thickens, 1 to 2 minutes. Ser

Gingered Pear Chi

A lovely, easy, but out-of-the-ordinary stir-fr

1 (16-oz.) can pear halves
About 1/4 cup water
1/2 cup ginger ale
1/4 cup packed brown sugar
3 tablespoons soy sauce
4 chicken breast halves, skinned, boned

Drain pear halves, reserving juice in a 1-cu
In a small bowl, combine juice mixture, g
chicken into 3/4-inch pieces. Heat oil in w
firm and white, 5 to 7 minutes. Add ginge
Stirring occasionally, simmer over mediur
starch, 1/4 cup water and salt to taste. Stir i
utes. Add pear halves and nuts. Stir occasion

Pork, Lamb & Veal

Meat cooked in the wok is tender because it cooks very quickly. Long cooking toughens meat. Beef, veal and lamb can be eaten rare, but pork must be thoroughly cooked. This doesn't take long in the wok. In the following recipes, pork is stir-fried, then simmered until it is thoroughly cooked.

Stir-frying meat over high heat sears the surface, sealing in its natural juices. Before you sear any meat, wipe it dry or coat it with flour or cornstarch. Don't crowd the meat in the pan. Too much meat cooked at the same time cools the pan, causing the meat to turn a gray color and lose moisture. To stir-fry pork, heat a small amount of oil in your wok, then add a few pork strips at a time. Sear them on one side until juices rise to the surface, then quickly turn and sear the other side.

Feeling adventuresome? Let your imagination carry you away to North Africa where they use local grains to extend meat to feed a large population. Couscous with Lamb & Apricots is a simplified version of a North-African dish. Couscous can be cooked into a simple porridge or used to thicken stews or soups made with meat. Sweetened and mixed with fruit, it becomes a delicious dessert.

Still feeling adventuresome but want an easy-to-prepare meal? Try Köfta & Lentils. It is a classic Middle-Eastern lamb meatball dish containing tender lentils, steamed potatoes and stir-fried zucchini and celery. If ground lamb is not available, use ground lean beef instead. All are combined in the wok and simmered in a rich tomato mixture. It serves six or more people.❖

Buffet for a Crowd

Chilled Steamed Shrimp, page 77
Avery Island Shrimp Dip, page 137
Köfta & Lentils, page 107
Indonesian Twice-Fried Chicken, page 23
Chilled, Steamed Fresh-Vegetable Platter, page 42
Cherry-Cheese Pie, page 149
Coffee

Alsace-Lorraine Stir-Fry

The gin evaporates, leaving the traditional flavor of juniper berries.

2 or 3 smoked pork chops (about 1/2 lb.)
3 tablespoons oil
1/4 cup Vegetable Broth, page 133,
   or water
1 (16-oz.) can sauerkraut
1 medium onion, chopped
2 crisp tart apples, peeled, chopped
8 frankfurters, cut in
   1/2-inch diagonal slices

1 tablespoon light brown sugar
1/2 teaspoon dry mustard
1/2 cup Vegetable Broth, page 133,
   or water
1/2 cup dry gin
1/2 teaspoon coarsely ground black pepper
1/2 teaspoon ground cloves

Remove bones and fat from pork chops. Cut meat into 1/4-inch strips. Heat 1 tablespoon oil in wok over high heat. Add pork strips; stir-fry 1 minute. Reduce heat to low. Pour in 1/4 cup broth or water. Cover wok; simmer until liquid has evaporated, about 10 minutes. While pork simmers, pour sauerkraut into a colander. Remove brine by gently lifting and stirring sauerkraut with your hands while holding under cold running water. Drain well. Pat dry with paper towels; set aside. Spoon cooked pork strips into a medium bowl; set aside. Wipe wok dry with paper towels. Heat remaining 2 tablespoons oil in wok over high heat. Add onion and apples. Stir-fry 1 minute. Add frankfurters and cooked pork strips. Stir-fry 30 seconds. Add rinsed sauerkraut, brown sugar and dry mustard. Use 2 forks to lift and toss until distributed. Stir in remaining ingredients. Reduce heat to low. Cover wok; simmer 15 minutes. Remove cover; increase heat to high. Stir-fry until liquid has evaporated, 2 to 3 minutes. Makes 4 servings.

Caribbean Meatballs

Spicy meatballs in sauce can also be a tasty appetizer.

1 lb. ground lean pork
3/4 cup minced sun chokes or water chestnuts
1/2 cup minced green onions
1 (1-inch) cube gingerroot, minced
1 teaspoon soy sauce
1 egg, slightly beaten
1/3 cup cornstarch
Oil for deep frying

1 tablespoon oil
1 green pepper, cut in 1-inch squares
1/2 cup water
1/2 cup orange juice
1/2 cup chili sauce
1 tablespoon soy sauce
2 tablespoons honey
3 cups hot cooked rice

In a large bowl, combine pork, sun chokes or water chestnuts, green onions, ginger, 1 teaspoon soy sauce and egg. Shape into 1-inch balls. Roll meatballs in cornstarch. Pour oil for deep frying into wok until 1-1/2 inches deep in center. Heat oil to 350F (175C). Add meatballs to hot oil a few at a time. Cook until browned on all sides, 3 to 4 minutes. Drain on paper towels. Pour oil from wok. Wipe wok with paper towels. Heat 1 tablespoon oil in wok over high heat. Add green pepper. Stir-fry until crisp-tender, about 1 minute. Reduce heat to low. Add browned meatballs and water. Cover wok; simmer 20 minutes or until meatballs are cooked through center. In a small bowl, combine orange juice, chili sauce, 1 tablespoon soy sauce and honey. Pour over meatballs. Cook 2 minutes longer. Serve over rice. Makes 4 to 6 servings.

Pork & Cannellini Sicilian-Style

You'll think you're in Napoli.

4 rib pork chops, 1/2 inch thick
Salt and pepper to taste
1/4 cup all-purpose flour
1 tablespoon oil
2 garlic cloves, crushed
1 bay leaf
1/2 cup Chicken Broth, page 134, or
   Vegetable Broth, page 133
1/4 cup white wine

1/2 teaspoon dried leaf oregano, crumbled
1/2 teaspoon dried leaf basil, crumbled
1/2 teaspoon salt
1/4 teaspoon pepper
1 (20-oz.) can cannellini or
   white kidney beans, drained
1 (8-oz.) can tomato sauce
2 green onions, thinly sliced

Cut bones and fat from pork chops. Place boned chops between 2 pieces of waxed paper. Pound with a rolling pin or side of a heavy cleaver until 1/4 inch thick. Cut flattened chops into 1/2-inch strips. Sprinkle with salt and pepper to taste. Roll meat strips in flour. Shake briskly to remove excess flour. Stirring occasionally, heat oil, garlic and bay leaf in wok over low heat until lightly browned. Discard garlic and bay leaf. Increase heat to high. When oil is hot but not smoking, add flour-coated meat strips. Stir-fry until lightly browned, 3 to 4 minutes. Stir in broth, wine, oregano, basil, 1/2 teaspoon salt and 1/4 teaspoon pepper. Cover wok; simmer 10 minutes. Remove cover. Stir-fry until most of liquid has evaporated, 4 to 5 minutes. Add beans and tomato sauce. Stir until hot, 1 to 2 minutes. Garnish with green onions. Makes 4 servings.

Southern-Style Pork & Vegetables

A complete dinner prepared all at once in your wok.

3 tablespoons brown sugar
1 tablespoon cornstarch
1 teaspoon salt
2 tablespoons vinegar
3/4 cup Chicken Broth, page 134, or
   Vegetable Broth, page 133
1 tablespoon oil
2 loin pork chops, 1/2 inch thick
Salt and pepper to taste

2 slices mild onion, 1/4 inch thick
2 center slices firm tart apple,
   peeled, cored
About 1/2 lb. broccoli,
   cut in half lengthwise
2 slices canned sweet potatoes,
   1/2 inch thick
1 teaspoon salt

In a small saucepan, cook and stir brown sugar, cornstarch, 1 teaspoon salt, vinegar and broth over medium heat until thickened. Set aside. Heat oil in wok over high heat. Sprinkle chops with salt and pepper to taste. Brown on both sides in hot oil. Drain on paper towels. Pour oil from wok. Wipe wok with paper towels. Place a rack in wok. Pour in water until 1 inch below rack. Bring to a gentle boil over medium heat. Place browned chops in center of a 10" x 6" glass baking dish. Top each chop with an onion slice, then an apple slice. Pour brown-sugar sauce over chops. Place dish on rack. Cover wok. Steam 30 minutes, basting chops every 10 minutes with brown-sugar sauce. Place broccoli and sweet potato slices on opposite sides of pork chops. Sprinkle with 1/2 teaspoon salt and baste with some of sauce. Add boiling water to wok if necessary. Cover wok. Steam 10 minutes longer or until broccoli is tender. Makes 2 servings.

Napa Valley Stir-Fry

The green bulb-like stem of young kohlrabi tastes like a sweet, tender turnip.

2 large navel oranges
Water
4 rib pork chops, boned, fat removed
1/2 teaspoon salt
1/4 teaspoon pepper
1/4 cup all-purpose flour
1/2 cup oil
1 tablespoon oil
1 large onion, chopped

1 small kohlrabi, thinly sliced, if desired
1/2 cup Chicken Broth, page 134, or
   Vegetable Broth, page 133
2 teaspoons cornstarch
2 tablespoons honey
1/2 teaspoon orange extract
1/4 cup freshly minced parsley
3 cups hot cooked rice

Cut a thin layer of peel from 1 orange. Cut peel into slivers. In a small saucepan, cover orange peel with water. Bring to a boil over medium heat. Simmer 15 minutes. Drain and set aside. Cut remaining peel and white pith from both oranges. Cut oranges into 1/2-inch slices. Cut slices in half; set aside. Place each pork chop between 2 pieces of waxed paper. Pound with a rolling pin or side of a heavy cleaver until 1/4 inch thick. Cut flattened chops into 2-inch-wide strips. Sprinkle with salt and pepper. Rub flour into each strip. Shake off excess flour. Heat 1/2 cup oil in wok over medium heat. Add meat strips. Stir-fry until golden brown, 3 to 4 minutes; set aside. Pour oil from wok. Wipe wok with paper towels. Heat 1 tablespoon oil in wok over medium-high heat. Add onion and kohlrabi, if desired. Stir-fry 1 minute. Combine broth, cornstarch, honey and orange extract. Pour over onion mixture. Add browned meat. Cover wok; simmer 2 to 3 minutes. Stir in orange slices and parsley. Serve immediately over rice. Makes 4 servings.

How to Make Napa Valley Stir-Fry

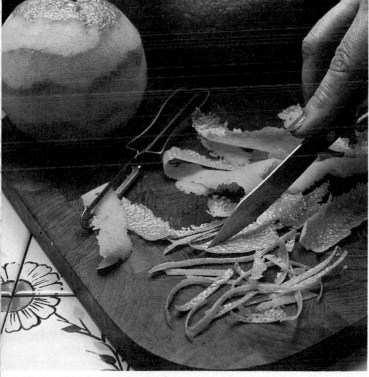

1/Cut a thin layer of peel from 1 orange, being careful not to get any white pith. Cut peel into slivers.

2/Roll pork strips in flour. Use your fingers to rub flour into each strip. Briskly shake off excess flour.

South-African Lamb Pilaf

Deliciously different, eye-pleasing and easy to prepare.

1 cup dried apples
1/2 cup dried pitted prunes
1/3 cup chopped dried apricots
1/2 cup raisins
1/2 cup orange juice
1 cup hot water
1 lb. ground lean lamb
1/2 cup dry breadcrumbs
1/4 cup milk
1 egg, slightly beaten
1 teaspoon salt
1/2 teaspoon paprika

1/4 cup all-purpose flour
Oil for deep-frying
1 medium onion, finely chopped
1 tablespoon curry powder
2 tablespoons red wine vinegar
1 tablespoon sugar
1 teaspoon tomato paste or ketchup
Salt to taste
Hot cooked bulgar or hot cooked rice
1 large banana, sliced
1/2 cup chopped dry-roasted peanuts

In a large bowl, combine apples, prunes, apricots and raisins. Add orange juice and water. Let stand at room temperature 1 to 2 hours. In a large bowl, combine lamb, breadcrumbs, milk, egg, 1 teaspoon salt and paprika. Shape into 1-inch balls. Roll meatballs in flour. Shake off excess flour. Pour oil for deep-frying into wok until 1-1/2 inches deep in center. Heat oil to 350F (175C). Fry meatballs, a few at a time, in hot oil until lightly browned on all sides, 3 to 4 minutes. Drain on paper towels; set aside. Pour all but 2 tablespoons oil from wok. Add onion; stir-fry 1 minute. Reduce heat to low. Stir in curry powder until fragrant, 1 to 2 minutes. Add soaked fruits and 1 cup of soaking liquid. Stir in vinegar and sugar. Add cooked meatballs, pushing them down into liquid. Cover wok; simmer 20 minutes. Stir in tomato paste or ketchup. Stir until liquid thickens, 1 to 2 minutes. Add salt to taste. Spoon bulgar or rice onto a large platter. Top with lamb mixture. Garnish with banana slices. Sprinkle with peanuts. Makes 6 servings.

Couscous with Lamb & Apricots

A delicious and simplified version of a North-African dish.

1 tablespoon oil
1 onion, finely chopped
1 lb. ground lean lamb
1/2 cup chopped dried apricots
1/2 cup slivered almonds

2 cups water
2 tablespoons butter, room temperature
1/2 teaspoon salt
1 cup couscous (semolina wheat cereal)
Freshly minced parsley

Heat oil in wok over high heat. Add onion; stir-fry 30 seconds. Add lamb. Stirring constantly, cook until meat is no longer pink. Spoon off fat as it accumulates. Add apricots, almonds, water, butter and salt. Bring to a rolling boil over high heat. Gradually stir in couscous. Stirring occasionally, boil until most of liquid is absorbed. Remove wok from heat. Cover and let stand 10 minutes or until all liquid is absorbed. Use a fork to fluff. Sprinkle with minced parsley. Makes 6 servings.

South-African Lamb Pilaf

Pizziaolo

Stir-fried steak Italian-style.

1 lb. lean top or bottom round steak,
  1 inch thick
2 tablespoons oil
2 medium onions, thinly sliced
3 green peppers, cut in 1/4-inch strips
2 large tomatoes, seeded, chopped
1/2 teaspoon salt
Pinch coarsely ground black pepper

1/2 teaspoon dried leaf basil, crushed
1/2 teaspoon Italian seasoning
1/4 teaspoon ground oregano
1 teaspoon red wine vinegar
2 tablespoons water
1/2 cup pitted whole ripe olives
3 cups hot cooked rice or 1 (8-oz.) pkg.
  broad flat noodles or other pasta, cooked

Cut meat into thin strips. Heat 1 tablespoon oil in wok over high heat. Stir-fry beef strips in hot oil only until no pink remains. Spoon cooked meat onto a warm platter; set aside. Reduce heat to medium. Add remaining tablespoon oil to wok. Add onions and green peppers. Stir-fry 2 minutes. Add tomatoes, salt, black pepper, basil, Italian seasoning and oregano. Stir-fry 1 minute. Add vinegar and water. Cover wok and simmer 1 minute. Add cooked meat and olives. Stir-fry until meat is hot, about 1 minute. Serve over rice, noodles or other pasta. Makes 4 servings.

Beef in Mustard Sauce

Steak lovers, this dish is for you!

1 lb. sirloin steak or
  other beef steak, 1-1/2 inches thick
2 tablespoons oil
6 or 8 thick green onions, cut in
  1-inch julienne strips
1/4 cup Quick Beef Broth, page 133, or
  Vegetable Broth, page 133

2 tablespoons Dijon-style mustard
1 tablespoon lemon juice
1/2 teaspoon salt
1 teaspoon coarsely ground black pepper
3 cups hot cooked rice

Cut steak into 1'' x 1/4'' strips. Heat 1 tablespoon oil in wok over high heat. Add beef strips. Stir-fry until medium-rare, 1 to 2 minutes. Place cooked meat on a warm platter. Heat remaining tablespoon oil in wok. Add green onions; stir-fry 1 minute. Add broth, mustard, lemon juice, salt and pepper. Bring to a rolling boil. Pour over steak. Serve over rice. Makes 4 servings.

How to Make Middle-East Curried-Beef Sandwich

1/Stir-fry beef until no longer pink. Add ingredients as instructed in recipe.

2/Cut each pita bread in half. Fill each pocket with hot meat mixture.

Middle-East Curried-Beef Sandwich

A hot sandwich for a lunch or an after-the-game supper.

1 tablespoon oil
1 large onion, chopped
1 garlic clove, minced
1 lb. ground lean beef
2 teaspoons curry powder or to taste
1 teaspoon salt

3 tablespoons chili sauce
1 teaspoon sugar
1 teaspoon vinegar
1 cup fresh bean or alfalfa sprouts
1/2 cup plain yogurt, room temperature
6 large pita breads, heated

Heat oil in wok over high heat. Add onion and garlic. Stir-fry 30 seconds. Add beef. Stir-fry until no longer pink, breaking up meat with a wooden spoon. Stir in curry powder, salt, chili sauce, sugar and vinegar. Add bean sprouts. Stir gently until hot. Set wok off heat to cool slightly. Reduce heat to low. Fold in yogurt. Gently stir over low heat until yogurt is hot. Cut each pocket bread in half. Fill pockets with hot meat mixture. Serve hot. Makes 6 servings.

Steak Mirabeau & Chateau Potatoes

Superb and unusual flavor that is quick and easy to prepare in your wok.

1 lb. lean top or bottom round steak,
  1 inch thick
12 small to medium new potatoes,
  uniform in size, peeled

1 tablespoon oil
2 tablespoons butter
1 (2-oz.) can anchovy fillets, drained
1/2 cup sliced pimiento-stuffed olives

Cut steak into thinnest possible strips; set aside. Place a rack in wok. Pour water into wok until 1 inch below rack. Bring to a gentle boil over medium heat. Place potatoes on rack. Cover wok. Steam potatoes until tender when pierced to center with a small knife, about 15 minutes. Set aside to cool. Drain water from wok. Wipe dry with paper towels. Heat oil in wok over high heat. Stir-fry beef strips in hot oil only until strips are no longer pink, about 5 minutes. Drain on paper towels. Cut cooled potatoes into halves or quarters. Reduce heat to medium. Melt butter in wok. Add potatoes. Gently stir until heated through, about 1 minute. Add cooked meat strips, anchovies and olives. Cook and gently stir only until meat is hot, 1 to 2 minutes. Makes 4 servings.

Marco Polo Beef & Noodles

You'll be reminded of Italian pasta with meat sauce.

Garnishes, see below
1 lb. ground lean beef
1 teaspoon Oriental sesame oil
1 medium onion, chopped
1/3 cup ketchup
1/4 cup soy sauce

1/4 teaspoon crushed dried hot red pepper
2 tablespoons mirin or
  2 tablespoons saké plus 1 tablespoon sugar
8 oz. linguine, cooked
Oriental sesame oil, if desired

Garnishes:
1/4 lb. mushrooms, thinly sliced
1 cup chopped green onions

1 cup bean sprouts
2 medium tomatoes

Prepare garnishes; set aside. Place wok over high heat. Add beef. Stir-fry until no pink remains. Turn into a colander over a medium bowl to drain. Spoon 1 tablespoon drippings from meat back into wok. Add 1 teaspoon sesame oil; heat until sizzling. Add onion; stir-fry over high heat 30 seconds. Reduce heat to medium. Stir in ketchup, soy sauce, red pepper and mirin or saké and sugar. Stir 1 minute or until hot. Add drained meat; stir to blend. Spoon a fourth of noodles into each of 4 small, deep bowls. Top each with a fourth of meat mixture. Place garnishes in separate small bowls. Serve noodles and beef with garnishes. To eat, sprinkle each serving with sesame oil, if desired. Makes 4 servings.

Garnishes:
Rinse bean sprouts. Place in a metal sieve. Lower into a pot of gently boiling water until completely covered. Blanch 1 minute. Rinse immediately in cold running water to stop cooking; set aside. Use a slotted spoon to lower tomatoes into gently boiling water. Leave in water 30 seconds. Immediately immerse in cold water to stop cooking. Use a small knife to remove peel. Cut peeled tomatoes in half; remove seeds. Coarsely chop tomatoes.

As-You-Like-It Stir-Fried Steak

Choose tender beef sirloin or less-tender round steak. Use the vegetable of your choice.

1-1/2 lbs. lean beef sirloin or
    beef fillet, or 1 lb. lean top or
    bottom round, 1 inch thick
3 tablespoons oil
3 medium zucchini, if desired,
    cut in 1" x 1/4" strips
2 cups diagonally sliced celery,
    1/8 inch thick, if desired

2 cups broccoli flowerets, if desired
2 tablespoons water
1/2 cup Mustard Sauce, Sauce Diable,
    Hoisin Steak Sauce, Worcestershire-
    Lemon Sauce or Soy-Sherry Sauce,
    all on page 140
3 cups hot cooked rice or noodles or
    4 thick slices French bread

Cut sirloin or fillet of beef into 1/4-inch slices, or cut round steak into thinnest possible slices. Heat 1 tablespoon oil in wok over high heat. If using thicker, more-tender strips of sirloin or fillet of beef, arrange a few strips in hot oil in a single layer. Quickly sear strips on both sides, turning once. Place on a warm plate. Add more oil to wok as needed. Repeat with remaining strips. If using thinner slices or less-tender round steak, add half of meat slices to hot oil. Stir-fry 30 seconds or until no longer pink. As meat is cooked, place on a warm platter; set aside. Repeat with another tablespoon oil and remaining meat slices. Heat remaining tablespoon oil in wok. Add desired vegetable; stir-fry 1 minute. Add water. Cover wok; simmer 30 seconds. Remove cover. Stir-fry until vegetable is crisp-tender. Add cooked meat. Stir in desired sauce. Stir-fry until liquid is hot and thickened. Serve over rice, noodles or French bread. Makes 4 to 6 servings.

South-of-the-Border Beef

Full of hearty flavor.

4 large ripe tomatoes
4 to 6 cups boiling water
1 tablespoon oil
2 medium onions, chopped
1 garlic clove, minced
1 (4-oz.) can diced green chilies
1 lb. ground lean beef
2 to 3 tablespoons water or Quick Beef
    Broth, page 133, if desired

8 to 10 pitted green olives, sliced
1 teaspoon dried leaf oregano, crushed
Salt to taste
Coarsely ground black pepper to taste
3 cups hot cooked rice or
    8 oz. noodles, cooked
1 cup shredded Monterey Jack cheese or
    American cheese (4 oz.)

Hold tomatoes in boiling water 1 minute. Quickly hold under cold running water to stop cooking. Remove peel. Remove and discard seeds. Coarsely chop tomatoes; set aside. Heat oil in wok over medium-high heat. Add onions, garlic and chilies. Stir-fry 1 minute. Add beef. Stir-fry until meat is no longer pink. Use a wooden spoon to break up meat. Add chopped tomatoes; stir-fry about 1 minute. Cover wok; simmer 5 minutes. If mixture seems dry, add water or broth 1 tablespoon at a time. Stir in olives, oregano and salt and pepper to taste. Spoon over rice or noodles. Sprinkle 1/4 cup cheese over each serving as it is spooned onto individual plates. Serve immediately. Makes 4 servings.

After-Work Stew

Chinese steaming and slicing speeds the cooking of this all-American dinner.

2 medium potatoes
1 large onion
2 medium carrots
1 lb. flank steak, 1 inch thick
2 tablespoons oil
2 stalks celery, cut in 1/2-inch slices
1 medium turnip, peeled, cut in thin wedges

1/4 cup Vegetable Broth, page 133
1 cup cooked peas
2 tablespoons Escoffier Sauce Robert or
   other thick steak sauce
1 teaspoon Dijon-style mustard
Salt and pepper to taste

Place a rack in wok. Pour water into wok until 1 inch below rack. Bring to a gentle boil over medium heat. While water comes to a boil, peel potatoes. Cut into 1-inch cubes. Place in a shallow 8- or 9-inch square baking dish. Place dish on rack. Loosely place a tent of foil over dish. Cover wok. Steam 15 minutes or until potatoes are tender; set aside. Pour water from wok. Wipe dry with paper towels. While potatoes cook, slice onion vertically into thin slices. Separate slices into strips. Scrape peel from carrots. Cut carrots into 1/4-inch diagonal slices. Set prepared vegetables aside. Cut steak across grain into 1/4-inch strips. Heat oil in wok over high heat. When almost sizzling, add steak strips. Stir-fry until no longer pink. Add onion strips, carrot slices, celery and turnip. Stir-fry 2 minutes. Add broth; bring to a boil. Add steamed potatoes and peas. Stir in steak sauce, mustard and salt and pepper to taste. Makes 4 servings.

How to Make After-Work Stew

1/After steaming potatoes, pour water from wok. Wipe dry with paper towels.

2/Slice onion vertically into thin slices. Separate slices into strips.

Beef & Bean Curd Chili

Weight watchers take note—this chili is low in calories.

2 tablespoons oil
1 small garlic clove, minced
1 medium white onion, finely chopped
1 small green pepper, finely chopped
2 to 3 tablespoons chili powder
1/2 teaspoon sugar
1/2 lb. ground lean beef
1/2 lb. tofu, cut in 1/2-inch cubes

1/2 cup Quick Beef Broth or
  Vegetable Broth, page 133
1 tablespoon soy sauce
1 tablespoon cornstarch
1/4 cup water
2 to 3 cups shredded iceberg lettuce or
  bok choy

Heat oil in wok over medium-high heat. Add garlic, onion and green pepper. Stir-fry 30 seconds. Stir in chili powder and sugar. Add beef. Stir-fry until meat is no longer pink. Break up beef with a wooden spoon. Add tofu, broth and soy sauce. Reduce heat to low. Simmer 5 minutes, stirring occasionally. Combine cornstarch and water. Stir into beef mixture until liquid thickens. To serve, spoon over lettuce or bok choy. Serve immediately. Makes 4 servings.

Beef & Vegetable Stir-Fry

Quick-cooking, beef-flavor soup noodles give this stir-fry double-beef flavor.

1 lb. lean top round of beef, 1 inch thick
2 tablespoons soy sauce
2 tablespoons brandy
1/3 cup cornstarch
2 tablespoons oil
1/4 lb. mushrooms, thinly sliced
1 (16-oz.) pkg. frozen Chinese-style
  vegetables

1/4 cup Quick Beef Broth or
  Vegetable Broth, page 133, or water
1 teaspoon cornstarch
2 tablespoons water
1/4 teaspoon sugar
2 cups water
1 (3-oz.) pkg. Oriental-style noodles with
  beef-flavor soup base

Cut beef into thin slices. Place in an 11" x 7" glass baking dish. Combine soy sauce and brandy. Pour over sliced beef. Let stand 30 minutes at room temperature. Drain, reserving marinade. Pat meat slices dry with paper towels. Rub cornstarch into marinated beef slices. Heat 1 tablespoon oil in wok over high heat. Add coated beef slices. Stir-fry until lightly browned, about 5 minutes. Place browned meat slices in a large bowl; set aside. Add remaining tablespoon oil to wok. Add mushrooms; stir-fry 30 seconds. Add frozen vegetables. Stir-fry until coated with oil. Pour in broth or 1/4 cup water. Cover wok. Simmer 3 minutes or until vegetables are crisp-tender. Use a slotted spoon to place cooked vegetables in bowl with browned meat; set aside. In a small bowl, combine 1 teaspoon cornstarch and 2 tablespoons water. Stir in sugar and 2 cups water. Pour into wok. Stir while bringing to a rolling boil over medium-high heat. Slowly add noodles, being sure water continues to boil. Reserve seasoning packet. Reduce heat to low. Cook and stir 3 minutes or until noodles are tender. Add cooked meat and vegetables. Stir in noodle seasonings. Gently stir until mixture is heated through, 1 to 2 minutes. Makes 6 servings.

Many Splendored Things

Y ou can put a recipe that includes chicken and seafood, or meat and chicken, plus many-splendored things in only one place—on a party menu. Whenever you prepare and serve any one of these splendid combinations, it *is* a party! Each recipe in this chapter is a classic, international favorite, ideally suited to entertaining.

Feature any one of them on the menu and your party can't help but be a success. What's more, you'll be a success, too. Each one is easy and quick to prepare in your wok, leaving you plenty of time to make all other party arrangements without being rushed.

The many-splendored things in this chapter have the convenience of combining foods as in a casserole, and save energy as well. There is no need to heat the oven. Each recipe cooks in very little time on top of a stove. The wok is more efficient than traditional pots and pans.

It is fun and easy to prepare and serve food from a wok at the table. An electric wok can be placed directly on a table or a conventional wok can be placed on a portable burner next to the serving table. If you don't have a portable burner, prepare the food on the stove top, then keep it warm over an alcohol burner or a candle.

Traditionally, paella is cooked in a two-handled casserole pan called a *paella*. The ingredients in Paella in a Wok are traditional—only the pan is different. Serve this elaborate paella from your wok, or if you prefer, spoon it into a casserole dish or onto a platter.❖

Buffet Supper
Thai Stuffed Chicken Wings, page 18
Batter-Fried Mini Drums, page 20
Paella in a Wok, page 125
Hearty Red Wine from Spain or California
Pillow-Puff Cookies, page 156
Coffee

Thailand Pork & Shrimp

An intriguing blend of flavors, colors and textures prepared in a minimum of time.

1 egg
1 teaspoon soy sauce
2 teaspoons oil
3 cups cold cooked rice
2 tablespoons oil
1 garlic clove, crushed
1 (1-inch) cube gingerroot, crushed
1 lb. lean pork, cut in julienne strips

2 anchovy fillets, drained, chopped
1/2 cup Quick Beef Broth, page 133,
   Vegetable Broth, page 133, or water
1 lb. medium shrimp, shelled, deveined
1/2 cup thinly sliced green onions
Crushed dried hot red pepper, if desired
1 cucumber, peeled, cut in julienne strips
1 tomato, cut in wedges

In a small bowl, beat egg with soy sauce; set aside. Heat 2 teaspoons oil in wok. Add rice. Stir-fry until hot. Add egg mixture. Stir fry until rice is coated with egg mixture and is dry. Turn out onto a platter. Set aside and keep hot. Heat 2 tablespoons oil in wok over low heat. Add garlic and ginger. Cook until lightly browned. Discard garlic and ginger. Increase heat to high. Add pork; stir-fry until no longer pink. Add anchovies and broth or water. Reduce heat to low. Cover wok. Simmer until most of liquid has evaporated, about 5 minutes. Add shrimp. Stir-fry until shrimp are firm and pink, about 2 minutes. Stir in green onions and red pepper. Spoon pork mixture over rice. Top with cucumber strips and tomato wedges. Makes 6 servings.

Paella in a Wok

This authentic paella is prepared to perfection in your wok.

1 (1-1/2- to 2-lb.) broiler-fryer, cut up
1/4 cup all-purpose flour
Oil for deep-frying
2 tablespoons oil
1 large onion, chopped
1 garlic clove, minced
1 teaspoon crushed dried hot red pepper
1 (1-lb.) can Italian plum tomatoes
1 cup dry white wine
1 teaspoon dried leaf oregano, crushed

1 teaspoon salt
18 small littleneck clams
1 lb. medium fresh or frozen shrimp,
   shelled, deveined
1 pint sea scallops, halved or quartered
1 (6-oz.) can artichoke hearts, drained
1 cup cooked green peas
1/2 cup sliced pimiento-stuffed olives
Saffron Rice, page 66

Wipe chicken pieces dry with paper towels. Roll in flour. Use your fingers to rub flour into each piece. Shake off excess flour. Pour oil for deep-frying into wok until 1-1/2 inches deep in center. Heat oil to 350F (175C). Fry chicken pieces in hot oil, a few at a time, until browned on all sides and juices run clear when meat is pierced with a fork, 15 to 20 minutes. Drain on paper towels; set aside. Pour oil from wok. Wipe with paper towels. Heat 2 tablespoons oil in wok over high heat. When hot but not smoking, add onion, garlic and red pepper. Stir-fry 1 minute. Add tomatoes with juice. Use a wooden spoon to cut whole tomatoes into pieces. Stir in wine, oregano and salt. Reduce heat to low. Cover wok; simmer 10 minutes. Add browned chicken and clams. Cover wok. Cook until clams open, about 5 minutes. Remove and discard any clams that do not open. Stir in shrimp, scallops, artichoke hearts, peas and olives. Cover wok. Simmer 2 minutes longer or until shrimp are pink and scallops are opaque. Add Saffron Rice. Toss to distribute. Serve from wok or spoon onto a large platter. Makes 6 to 8 servings.

Thailand Pork & Shrimp

Indonesian-Style Fried Noodles

Beautiful and festive one-dish party fare.

2 teaspoons cornstarch
1 tablespoon soy sauce
1 tablespoon dark corn syrup
1/4 cup boiling water
Pinch ground coriander
Dash coarsely ground black pepper
6 cups water
1 teaspoon salt
2 teaspoons oil

1 (8-oz.) pkg. vermicelli
2 tablespoons oil
1 large garlic clove, minced
1 cup shredded bok choy or romaine lettuce
1 (6-oz.) pkg. frozen tiny shrimp, thawed
1 cup slivered cooked chicken
1 cup crushed fried rice sticks or
    canned French-fried onions

In a small bowl, combine cornstarch, soy sauce and corn syrup. Stir in 1/4 cup boiling water, coriander and pepper; set aside. In a large saucepan, bring 6 cups water to a rapid boil over medium-high heat. Add salt and 1 teaspoon oil. Add vermicelli, being sure water continues to boil. Cook until still slightly firm, 3 to 5 minutes. Drain and turn into a large bowl. Add remaining teaspoon oil. Toss to coat noodles with oil; set aside. Heat 2 tablespoons oil in wok over medium heat. Add garlic; stir-fry 30 seconds. Add bok choy or lettuce; stir-fry until limp, about 30 seconds. Add shrimp and chicken. Stir in soy sauce mixture. Add drained noodles. Toss over medium heat until noodles are hot and coated with sauce. Divide noodle mixture among 4 plates or bowls. Sprinkle with crumbled rice sticks or French-fried onions. Makes 4 servings.

Puerto-Rican Guisado

Mixed seafood and meat stew. Fantastic!

1/2 lb. spicy sausage links or
    Italian sausage
Water
2 tablespoons oil
1 medium onion, chopped
1 garlic clove, minced
1 canned hot green or red pepper,
    finely chopped
1 lb. sole or haddock fillets,
    cut in 1/2-inch strips

1 pint scallops, halved or quartered
1/2 cup slivered cooked ham
1 frozen rock lobster tail, if desired,
    thawed, cut in 1/2-inch slices
1/2 cup Chicken Broth, page 134, or
    Vegetable Broth, page 133
1/2 teaspoon ground coriander
3 cups cold cooked rice
2 tablespoons freshly minced parsley
1 lemon or lime, cut in wedges

Place sausage in a small saucepan. Use a fork to prick sausage on all sides. Add water until 1/2 inch above sausage. Bring water to a gentle boil over medium heat. Reduce heat to low. Simmer 15 minutes to remove most of fat from sausage. Drain and cut into 1/4-inch slices. Heat oil in wok over high heat. Add sliced sausage. Stir-fry until crisp, about 5 minutes. Reduce heat to medium. Add onion, garlic and green or red pepper. Stirring occasionally, cook until onion is soft. Add fish, scallops, ham and lobster, if desired. Stir-fry 1 minute. Stir in broth and coriander. Cover wok; simmer 2 minutes or until fish is opaque. Add rice. Gently lift and mix with forks until rice is hot, 30 seconds. Add parsley; gently toss. Serve from wok or turn into a deep platter. Garnish with lemon or lime wedges. Makes 6 servings.

Mediterranean Chicken   Cover photo.

A very special dish for your next party.

1 large lemon	1 medium mild red onion, chopped
1 navel orange	1 garlic clove, minced
12 pitted ripe Greek olives	1/4 teaspoon powdered saffron, if desired
1 cup boiling water	1 teaspoon ground coriander
1/4 cup all-purpose flour	1-1/2 cups Chicken Broth, page 134, or
1/2 teaspoon salt	Vegetable Broth, page 133
1/4 teaspoon pepper	1/2 teaspoon salt
4 chicken thighs	1/4 teaspoon pepper
4 chicken legs	2 medium tomatoes, peeled, cut in wedges
1/2 cup oil	3 cups hot cooked rice
1 tablespoon oil	

Cut 4 thin slices from centers of lemon and orange. Use remaining lemon and orange for another purpose. Cut each slice into 4 wedges. In a small bowl, combine olives, lemon wedges and orange wedges. Pour in boiling water. Let steep 20 minutes. Drain; set fruit and olives aside. In a pie plate, combine flour, 1/2 teaspoon salt and 1/4 teaspoon pepper. Roll chicken pieces in flour mixture. Use your fingers to rub flour mixture into chicken pieces; shake off excess flour. Heat 1/2 cup oil in wok over medium-high heat. Fry chicken pieces, 3 or 4 at a time, in hot oil until golden brown, 6 to 8 minutes. Drain browned chicken on paper towels. Pour oil from wok. Wipe wok with paper towels. Heat 1 tablespoon oil in wok over medium-high heat. Add onion and garlic; stir-fry until onion is soft. Stir in saffron, if desired, coriander, broth, 1/2 teaspoon salt and 1/4 teaspoon pepper. Add browned chicken. Reduce heat to low. Cover wok; simmer until chicken is tender, about 20 minutes. Add lemon and orange wedges, olives and tomato wedges. Stir only until distributed. Serve with rice. Makes 4 servings.

Normandy Chicken

An elegant party dish with applejack flavor.

1 lb. chicken thighs, skinned, boned	2 tablespoons oil
2 tablespoons apple jelly	1 medium green pepper, cut in
1/4 cup applejack, apple brandy or cider	3/4-inch squares
1/4 cup Chicken Broth, page 134, or	1 cup walnut halves
Vegetable Broth, page 133	2 tart apples, coarsely chopped
1 tablespoon hoisin sauce or soy sauce	

Cut chicken into 3/4-inch pieces; set aside. In a small saucepan, combine apple jelly, applejack, brandy or cider, broth and hoisin sauce or soy sauce. Stir over medium heat until jelly dissolves; set aside. Heat oil in wok. Add chicken pieces. Stir-fry until meat is firm, 3 to 5 minutes. Add green pepper, walnuts and apples. Stir-fry until green pepper is crisp-tender, about 2 minutes. Stir in jelly mixture. Makes 4 servings.

North-African Couscous with Chicken

An easy one-dish party meal. Simply sensational.

1/4 cup all-purpose flour
1/2 teaspoon salt
4 chicken legs
4 chicken thighs
Oil for deep-frying
1 tablespoon oil
1 medium white onion, chopped
3 medium zucchini, peeled, cut in
   1/4-inch cubes

1 teaspoon ground turmeric
1 (16-oz.) can garbanzo beans
3 cups water
1 cup orange juice
1 tablespoon butter, room temperature
1/2 teaspoon salt
1 cup couscous (semolina wheat cereal)
1/2 cup raisins
1/2 cup slivered almonds

In a pie plate, combine flour and 1/2 teaspoon salt. Roll chicken pieces in flour mixture. Use your fingers to rub flour mixture into chicken pieces. Shake off excess flour. Pour oil for deep-frying into wok until 1-1/2 inches deep in center. Heat oil to 350F (175C). Fry coated chicken pieces in hot oil until golden brown and juices run clear when chicken is pierced with a fork, 15 to 20 minutes. Drain on paper towels; set aside. Pour oil from wok. Wipe wok with paper towels. Heat 1 tablespoon oil over high heat. Add onion and zucchini. Stir-fry 1 minute. Stir in turmeric, garbanzo beans, water, orange juice, butter and 1/2 teaspoon salt. Bring to a boil over high heat. Stir in couscous, raisins and almonds. Add chicken pieces. Spoon couscous mixture over chicken. Remove wok from heat. Cover wok. Let stand until all water has been absorbed by couscous, about 10 minutes. Makes 6 to 8 servings.

Louisiana Gumbo Stir-Fry

Filé powder is made from dried sassafras leaves. It adds authentic Creole flavor.

1 tablespoon oil
1 small onion, chopped
1 green pepper, chopped
1 garlic clove, minced
1 (16-oz.) bag frozen mixed gumbo vegetables
   or 1 cup each of frozen okra, frozen
   lima beans and frozen whole-kernel corn
1/4 cup water
1 (16-oz.) can tomatoes
1/4 teaspoon ground thyme

1/4 teaspoon ground basil
1/4 teaspoon ground tarragon
1/2 teaspoon salt
1/4 teaspoon black pepper
1 tablespoon tomato paste
1/2 lb. small shrimp, shelled, deveined
1 pint small oysters, drained
1/2 cup slivered, cooked lean ham
4-1/2 cups hot cooked rice
Filé powder, if desired

Heat oil in wok over medium-high heat. Add onion, green pepper and garlic. Stir-fry 1 minute. Add frozen vegetables. Stir-fry until coated with oil. Stir in water, tomatoes with juice, thyme, basil, tarragon, salt, black pepper and tomato paste. Reduce heat to low. Cover wok. Stirring occasionally, simmer until vegetables are crisp-tender, about 15 minutes. Stir in shrimp, oysters and ham. Cover wok. Simmer 2 minutes or until edges of oysters begin to curl and shrimp are firm and pink. Serve over rice. Sprinkle each serving with filé powder, if desired. Makes 6 to 8 servings.

Empress Chicken

Serve to true royalty—family and friends.

4 chicken breast halves, skinned, boned
1 tablespoon oil
1 garlic clove, crushed
1 (1-inch) cube gingerroot, crushed
1/2 cup dry white wine
1/4 lb. large mushrooms, quartered
1/2 cup thinly sliced celery
1/2 cup cooked green peas

1/2 cup diced, cooked lean ham
2 tablespoons soy sauce
1/2 cup Chicken Broth, page 134, or
    Vegetable Broth, page 133
2 teaspoons cornstarch
3 tablespoons water
1 (8-oz.) pkg. vermicelli, cooked

Cut chicken into 3/4-inch pieces; set aside. Pour oil into cold wok; add garlic and ginger. Place over low heat until garlic turns brown, 3 to 4 minutes. Remove and discard garlic and ginger. Increase heat to high. When sizzling, add chicken pieces. Stir-fry until chicken turns white and becomes firm. Reduce heat to medium-low. Add wine. Stirring often, simmer until wine evaporates. Add mushrooms and celery; stir-fry 1 minute. Add peas, ham, soy sauce and broth. Stir until hot, about 3 minutes. In a small bowl, combine cornstarch and water. Stir into chicken mixture. Cook and stir until liquid thickens. Serve over vermicelli. Makes 4 servings.

Linguine Primavera

A beautiful blend of fresh vegetables, pasta, ham and cheese.

2 large firm ripe tomatoes
1/2 lb. broccoli
2 tablespoons oil
1 garlic clove, crushed
1 small zucchini, thinly sliced
1/4 lb. mushrooms, thinly sliced
1/4 lb. lean baked ham, slivered
2 tablespoons minced fresh thyme or
    1 teaspoon dried leaf thyme
1/4 cup chopped fresh basil leaves or
    1 teaspoon dried leaf basil and
    1/4 cup minced parsley

3 tablespoons water
2 tablespoons fresh oregano or
    1 teaspoon dried leaf oregano
1 teaspoon minced canned hot red pepper or
    1/2 teaspoon crushed dried hot red pepper
1/2 lb. fresh peas, shelled, or
    1 cup frozen peas, thawed
1 teaspoon salt
1 teaspoon sugar
1 (8-oz.) pkg. linguine, cooked
1/2 cup grated Parmesan cheese (1-1/2 oz.)

Cut tomatoes in half. Remove seeds and juice. Cut tomato shells into narrow strips. Use paper towels to dry tomato strips; set aside. Trim broccoli, cutting off tough lower stem. Use your fingers to break off flowerets. Keeping stems separate from flowerets, cut stems lengthwise into narrow strips. Set broccoli flowerets and stem strips aside. Heat 2 tablespoons oil in wok over low heat. Add garlic; stir-fry until browned. Discard garlic. Increase heat to high. When oil starts to sizzle, add broccoli stem strips, zucchini and mushrooms. Stir-fry 2 minutes. Stir in ham, broccoli flowerets, thyme, basil or basil-parsley mixture, water, oregano, red pepper, peas, salt and sugar. Cover and simmer 1 minute. Remove cover; stir-fry until crisp-tender, 3 to 5 minutes. Stir in tomato strips, cooked linguine and cheese. Lift and stir until evenly distributed. Turn into a large serving bowl. Serve immediately. Makes 4 to 6 servings.

Fish Strips & Vegetable Platter

A beautiful platter of crisp-fried fish and colorful, stir-fried vegetables.

3 medium carrots
2 small white turnips
2 small zucchini
1 tablespoon oil
2 tablespoons water
1 teaspoon salt
1/2 teaspoon sugar
1 tablespoon butter, if desired

1 (16-oz.) pkg. frozen haddock, thawed
Salt and pepper to taste
1/4 cup all-purpose flour
Oil for deep-frying
2 tablespoons lemon juice
1 to 2 tablespoons Worcestershire sauce
1/4 cup freshly minced parsley

Scrape peel from carrots. Cut crosswise into 1-inch slices, then lengthwise into julienne strips. Peel and thinly slice turnips. Cut turnip slices into julienne strips. Cut zucchini crosswise into 1-inch slices, then lengthwise into thin slices. Heat 1 tablespoon oil in wok over high heat. Add carrot strips, turnip strips and zucchini slices. Stir-fry 1 minute. Add water, 1 teaspoon salt and sugar; stir once. Cover wok; simmer 1 minute. Remove cover. Stir-fry until all liquid evaporates and vegetables are crisp-tender, 2 to 3 minutes. Stir in butter, if desired. Heat a large platter. Spoon vegetables around edge of heated platter, leaving center of platter open; keep warm. Wipe wok with paper towels. Cut fish into 2-inch strips. Sprinkle with salt and pepper to taste. Roll fish strips in flour. Use your fingers to rub flour into strips. Shake off excess flour. Pour oil for deep-frying into wok until 1-1/2 inches deep in center. Heat oil to 375F (190C). Fry fish strips in hot oil, a few at a time, until crisp and golden brown, about 1 minute. Drain on paper towels. Arrange fried fish in center of vegetables on platter. Sprinkle fish with lemon juice, Worcestershire sauce and parsley. Makes 4 servings.

Oriental Birthday Noodle Dish

In China, noodles are said to bring good luck and long life.

2 tablespoons chunky-style peanut butter
1/2 cup hot water
1 teaspoon brown sugar
2 tablespoons cornstarch
3 tablespoons soy sauce
2 tablespoons rice wine or dry sherry
2 teaspoons crushed dried hot red pepper
1-1/2 cups Chicken Broth, page 134, or
    Vegetable Broth, page 133

2 tablespoons oil
1 cup shredded bok choy or romaine lettuce
1 cup cooked green peas
3/4 cup slivered cooked ham
1 (6-oz.) pkg. frozen tiny shrimp, thawed,
1 (8-oz.) pkg. fine noodles, cooked
1 cup fresh bean sprouts
3/4 cup chopped green onions

In a medium bowl, stir peanut butter and hot water until smooth. Stir in brown sugar, cornstarch, soy sauce, rice wine or sherry, red pepper and broth; set aside. Heat oil in wok over high heat. Add bok choy or lettuce, peas, ham and shrimp. Stir-fry until hot, about 1 minute. Stir in noodles and bean sprouts. Stir-fry until hot. Sprinkle with green onions. Makes 6 servings.

How to Make Fish Strips & Vegetable Platter

1/Cut vegetables into thin, narrow strips. These are called *julienne strips* or *matchstick pieces.*

2/Fry fish strips in hot oil, a few at a time, until crisp and golden brown. Drain on paper towels.

Stir-Fried Shrimp in the Shell

Fun to eat and almost no work for the cook. Everyone peels his own shrimp.

1-1/2 lbs. jumbo shrimp in shell
1 garlic clove, crushed
1 (1-inch) cube gingerroot, crushed
3 tablespoons soy sauce

3 tablespoons dry sherry
1 teaspoon sugar
2 tablespoons oil

To prepare shrimp, use a small, sharp knife or kitchen shears to split shell along back of each shrimp. Do not remove shell. With tip of knife, remove vein. Rinse shrimp under cold running water. Pat dry with paper towels; set aside. In a large bowl, combine garlic, ginger, soy sauce, sherry and sugar. Add cleaned shrimp in shells; toss to coat evenly. Refrigerate 3 to 4 hours, turning shrimp in marinade occasionally. Drain shrimp. Heat oil in wok over high heat. Add drained shrimp. Stir and toss until shells are lightly browned, about 5 minutes. Serve hot or cold as an appetizer or as part of an Oriental-style buffet supper. Makes 6 servings.

Broths & Sauces

Vegetable Broth, fragrant, flavorful, quick, and easy to prepare, may become a staple in your kitchen as it has in mine. Unlike canned broth or broth made from bouillon cubes, it has no preservatives and, if you like, can be prepared with little or no salt. It's usually made from those end pieces of vegetables you might otherwise throw away. You may have more of one ingredient than another, or you may be lacking an ingredient. Don't worry. Use what you have.

Use Vegetable Broth in cooking instead of other liquid. And be sure to try it as a clear, no-calorie soup. It's full of vitamins and minerals. I've also given you a recipe for Quick Beef Broth. You can make this flavorful broth in less than 15 minutes. Chicken Broth is just as good, but takes a little longer to prepare.

The sauces that follow are toil- and trouble-free. Like all wok-cooked food, it is hard to believe something this easy to prepare can have so much flavor and savor. Use them in the recipes that call for them, but also use them to enrich and enhance any dish you prepare, any menu you plan, any meal you cook.

Use Make-Ahead Sauce for Stir-Frying whenever you prepare your own improvised stir-fry. It will replace any cornstarch mixture that contains beef or chicken broth, soy sauce, wine or sherry.❖

Vegetarian Luncheon
Mugs of Steamy Hot Vegetable Broth, page 133
Cheese Straws
Vegetable Paella, page 35
Small Bowl of Soy Sauce
Sugar-Free Sweet & Sour Sauce, page 139
Banana Fritters, page 146
Coffee

Vegetable Broth

Flavor-plus. Contains little or no salt and is almost calorie-free.

3 or 4 celery stalks
1 or 2 small onions, unpeeled
1 garlic clove, unpeeled
3 or 4 mushrooms or equivalent
    mushroom stems
1 ripe tomato or equivalent end pieces
2 or 3 parsley sprigs or
    equivalent parsley stems

1-1/2 qts. water
1/2 to 1 cup dry white wine or
    1/4 to 1/2 cup dry sherry, if desired
Crushed dried hot red peppers to taste
Dried leaf basil or fresh basil to taste
Dried leaf thyme or fresh thyme to taste
2 or 3 slivers lemon peel
Salt and pepper to taste, if desired

Combine all ingredients in a large saucepan. Bring to a rolling boil, then simmer 1 hour over low heat. Cool slightly. Strain; reserve broth. For a clear broth, line a fine sieve with cheesecloth. Pour vegetable mixture into lined sieve. Lightly press with your hands to extract as much liquid as possible. Pour strained broth into 1- or 2-cup containers with tight-fitting lids. Refrigerate up to 7 days or freeze up to 6 months. Makes about 4 cups.

Quick Beef Broth

Use the meat left from making this broth in South-of-the-Border Beef, page 120.

1 tablespoon oil
1/2 lb. ground lean beef
3 cups salt-free Vegetable Broth, above

1/2 cup dry sherry
Salt, if desired
Soy sauce, if desired

Heat oil in a large saucepan over medium heat. Add beef. Cook and stir until meat is no longer pink. Add broth and sherry. Bring to a boil. Turn heat to low. Simmer 30 minutes. If desired, season to taste with salt or soy sauce. Strain; reserve broth. Use meat for another purpose. Pour strained broth into 1- or 2-cup containers with tight-fitting lids. Refrigerate up to 7 days or freeze up to 6 months. Or pour into divided ice trays. Place in freezer until frozen. Store frozen cubes in a plastic bag in freezer. Makes about 3 cups.

Dashi

Japanese basic broth.

1 (4- to 5-inch) strip kelp (konbu)
About 1/4 cup loosely packed,
    dried bonito flakes (katsuo bushi)

5 cups water

In a large saucepan, combine all ingredients. Bring to a boil over medium-high heat. Immediately remove and discard kelp. Turn heat to low. Simmer 1 to 2 minutes. Line a colander with a double thickness of cheesecloth or a paper coffee filter. Place colander over a medium bowl. Pour broth mixture into lined colander. Reserve broth. Use Dashi immediately or pour into 1- or 2-cup containers with tight-fitting lids. Refrigerate and use within 5 days. Makes about 4-1/2 cups.

Chicken Broth

Parboiling the bones reduces the foam and gives you a better flavor.

About 1 lb. chicken bones with some meat,
   cooked or uncooked
Cold water
1 large onion, chopped
1 garlic clove
1 celery stalk, chopped
1/2 cup chopped mushroom stems

2 to 3 parsley sprigs
1 bay leaf
1/2 teaspoon dried leaf thyme
1 cup dry white wine or vermouth
9 to 10 cups water
Salt, if desired

Place chicken bones in a large pot. Add cold water to cover. Bring to a boil over high heat. Drain immediately. Rinse bones under cold running water. Drain thoroughly. Clean pot. Add rinsed bones and remaining ingredients. Bring to a boil over high heat. Turn heat to low. Simmer 2 hours. Strain broth through a fine sieve or colander. Discard bone mixture. Refrigerate broth 2 hours or until fat congeals on surface. Remove and discard fat. Pour broth into 1- or 2-cup containers with tight-fitting lids. Refrigerate up to 7 days or freeze up to 6 months. Or pour broth into divided ice trays. Place in freezer until frozen. Store frozen cubes in a plastic bag in freezer. Makes about 7 cups.

How to Make Chicken Broth

1/Combine bones and remaining ingredients. Bring to a boil. Simmer 2 hours. Strain. Chill broth. Discard fat.

2/Broth may be frozen in divided ice trays. Store frozen cubes in a plastic bag in freezer to use as needed.

Rémoulade Sauce

Louisiana's favorite. Use this highly seasoned sauce sparingly.

1 tablespoon freshly grated or
  prepared horseradish
1 tablespoon chopped celery
1 tablespoon chopped sour gherkins
1 tablespoon capers, drained
1 tablespoon Dijon-style mustard
1 tablespoon lemon juice

2 tablespoons ketchup
2 or 3 drops hot pepper sauce
1 teaspoon Worcestershire sauce
2 cups mayonnaise
Freshly ground black pepper to taste
Salt to taste

In a medium bowl, combine all ingredients. Refrigerate until chilled. Makes 2-1/2 cups.

Sauce Romanoff

The ultimate dip.

1 cup mayonnaise
1 tablespoon lemon juice
1 tablespoon freshly grated or
  prepared horseradish

1/2 cup dairy sour cream
1 (1-1/2-oz.) jar red salmon caviar

In a small bowl, combine mayonnaise, lemon juice, horseradish and sour cream. Refrigerate until chilled. Just before serving, gently fold in caviar. Makes about 1-3/4 cups.

Sweet & Sour Hoisin Sauce

Excellent with Indonesian Twice-Fried Chicken, page 23.

1/4 cup Vegetable Broth, page 133
1 (6-oz.) can unsweetened pineapple juice
1 tablespoon hoisin sauce

1/4 cup apricot jam
2 teaspoons cornstarch
2 tablespoons water

In a small saucepan, combine broth, pineapple juice, hoisin sauce and jam. Stir cornstarch into water until dissolved. Stir into broth mixture. Cook and stir over medium heat until thickened. Makes about 1-1/4 cups.

Make-Ahead Sweet & Sour Sauce

Use as a sauce with stir-fried pork, chicken, beef or vegetable dishes.

2 cups Vegetable Broth, page 133
1 (6-oz.) can frozen lemonade concentrate
1/4 cup ketchup

2 tablespoons soy sauce
1/4 cup Vegetable Broth, page 133
3 tablespoons cornstarch

In a medium saucepan, combine 2 cups broth, lemonade concentrate, ketchup and soy sauce. Bring to a simmer over medium-high heat. In a small bowl, combine 1/4 cup broth and cornstarch. Stir into lemonade mixture until slightly thickened. Pour into 1- or 2-cup containers with tight-fitting lids. Refrigerate 7 to 14 days or freeze up to 3 months. Or pour into divided ice trays. Place in freezer until frozen, 3 to 4 hours. Store frozen cubes in a plastic bag in freezer to use as needed. Makes about 3-1/2 cups.

Make-Ahead Sauce for Stir-Frying

Use this sauce as a substitute for combinations of broth, soy sauce and wine.

1/2 cup Vegetable Broth, page 133
1/2 cup cornstarch
2 cups boiling Vegetable Broth, page 133
1/2 cup soy sauce

1/2 cup dry sherry
3 tablespoons dark brown sugar
3 tablespoons rice wine vinegar or
　　white wine vinegar

Stir 1/2 cup broth into cornstarch; set aside. In a large bowl, combine 2 cups boiling broth, soy sauce, sherry and brown sugar. Stir in cornstarch mixture. Continue to stir until cornstarch and sugar have dissolved. Pour into 1- or 2-cup containers with tight-fitting lids. Refrigerate 7 to 14 days or freeze up to 3 months. Or pour into divided ice trays. Place in freezer until frozen, 3 to 4 hours. Store frozen cubes in a plastic bag in freezer to use as needed. Makes about 3-1/4 cups.

Lemon Sauce for Vegetables

Lovely, light, lemony flavor.

1 lemon
1 cup Vegetable Broth, page 133
1/3 cup sugar
1/3 cup cider vinegar

1/2 teaspoon soy sauce
2 teaspoons cornstarch
2 tablespoons water

Thinly slice lemon. Cut each slice into 4 wedges. In a small saucepan, combine lemon wedges, broth, sugar and vinegar. Simmer over low heat 30 minutes. In a small bowl, combine soy sauce, cornstarch and water. Stir into sauce mixture. Cook and stir until sauce is slightly thickened. Makes about 1-1/2 cups.

Low-Calorie Anchovy Cream

Only 17 calories per tablespoon. Delicious on vegetables.

1 cup low-fat cottage cheese
3 tablespoons lemon juice

2 or 3 anchovy fillets, drained, minced
1 to 2 drops hot pepper sauce, if desired

In blender or food processor, combine all ingredients; blend until smooth. Serve hot or cold. Makes about 1 cup.

Quick Curry Sauce for Vegetables

Use only a small dollop of this strong-flavored sauce on each vegetable serving.

1 (8-oz.) carton pineapple yogurt
1/2 cup mayonnaise
1 tablespoon lemon-flavor gelatin powder

2 to 3 teaspoons curry powder
1/2 teaspoon salt

In a small bowl, combine all ingredients; blend well. Refrigerate until chilled. Serve cold with hot or cold steamed vegetables. Makes about 1-1/2 cups.

Tartar Sauce

The perfect complement for fish or seafood.

1 hard-cooked egg yolk, mashed
1/4 cup cider vinegar
1 teaspoon Dijon-style mustard
2 cups mayonnaise

1 tablespoon chopped sour pickle
1 tablespoon capers, drained
Salt to taste

In a small bowl, combine all ingredients. Refrigerate until chilled. Makes about 2-1/3 cups.

Avery Island Shrimp Dip   Photo on page 13.

The perfect dip for Sesame Shrimp Chips, page 17.

1 cup ketchup
2 tablespoons prepared horseradish
2 tablespoons lemon juice

1 teaspoon Worcestershire sauce
4 or 5 drops Tabasco sauce

Combine all ingredients in a medium bowl; blend well. Refrigerate 30 minutes or until chilled. Makes about 1-1/4 cups.

Indonesian Dipping Sauce

Use as a pungent dipping sauce with Indonesian Twice-Fried Chicken, page 23.

1 cup packed dark brown sugar
1 cup water
1 cup soy sauce
1/4 cup dark molasses

1 teaspoon freshly grated gingerroot
1/2 teaspoon ground coriander
1/2 teaspoon freshly ground black pepper

Combine sugar and water in a 2-quart saucepan. Stir constantly over medium heat until sugar dissolves. Increase heat to high. Continue cooking until syrup reaches 200F (95C), about 5 minutes. Reduce heat to low. Stir in remaining ingredients. Cook and stir 3 minutes. Makes 3 cups.

Lemon-Butter Dip

Serve with seafood or crisp-tender vegetables.

1/2 cup butter
1/4 cup lemon juice

2 to 3 drops hot pepper sauce

In a small saucepan, melt butter over low heat. Stir in lemon juice and hot pepper sauce. Serve warm. Makes about 3/4 cup.

Mild & Mellow Garlic Butter

Gives just a touch of garlic to vegetables or casseroles.

1 tablespoon olive oil or vegetable oil
3 garlic cloves, crushed
1/2 cup butter

Salt to taste
3 drops hot pepper sauce, if desired

Heat oil in a small skillet over low heat. Add garlic. Stirring occasionally, cook until garlic is soft. Do not let garlic brown. Remove and discard garlic. Add butter to skillet. When melted, season with salt to taste and hot pepper sauce, if desired. Makes about 1/2 cup.

Piquant Dipping Sauce

Use this pleasantly pungent sauce with any kind of meat.

1/2 cup cider vinegar
1 cup packed light brown sugar
1 cup ketchup

2 tablespoons cornstarch
1/2 cup Chicken Broth, page 134,
    Vegetable Broth, page 133, or water

In a small saucepan, bring vinegar and sugar to a boil. Reduce heat to low; simmer 5 minutes. Stir in ketchup. Combine cornstarch and broth or water. Stir into vinegar mixture until thickened, about 2 minutes. Serve warm or at room temperature. Makes about 2 cups.

Lemony Mayonnaise

To each serving of salad, vegetables or seafood, add a dollop of this spicy sauce.

1 cup mayonnaise
2 tablespoons lemon juice

2 or 3 drops hot pepper sauce
2 or 3 drops Angostura Bitters, if desired

In a small bowl, combine all ingredients; blend well. Refrigerate until chilled. Makes about 1 cup.

Sweet & Sour Sauce

If you use sweetened pineapple juice, omit the sugar.

1/4 cup cold water
2 tablespoons cornstarch
1 cup unsweetened pineapple juice
3 tablespoons sugar

1/4 cup white vinegar
3 tablespoons ketchup
1 tablespoon soy sauce

Combine water and cornstarch; set aside. In a small saucepan, combine remaining ingredients. Stir over low heat until hot, 3 to 5 minutes. Stir in cornstarch mixture until sauce thickens slightly, about 2 minutes. Serve warm or at room temperature. Makes about 1-1/2 cups.

Sugar-Free Sweet & Sour Sauce

Excellent with stir-fried pork, chicken or vegetables.

1 (18-oz.) can unsweetened pineapple juice
1 (8-oz.) can tomato sauce
1/4 cup rice wine vinegar

3 tablespoons cornstarch
2 drops hot pepper sauce
Salt to taste

In a large saucepan, combine pineapple juice and tomato sauce. Gently stir over medium heat until hot. Stir vinegar into cornstarch. Stir into pineapple juice mixture until thickened, 2 to 3 minutes. Stir in hot pepper sauce and salt to taste. Makes 3-1/2 cups.

Chinese Mustard

Use this tangy sauce with Chinese Steamed Dumplings, page 27, or Western Won Tons, page 22.

1/4 cup dry white wine, beer or water
2 tablespoons dry mustard

In a small saucepan, heat wine, beer or water over medium heat. Stir mustard into hot liquid. Let stand 30 minutes to cool and develop flavor. Makes about 1/4 cup.

Stir-Fry Steak Sauces

Any of these sauces will complement As-You-Like-It Stir-Fried Steak, page 120.

Soy-Sherry Sauce

1 teaspoon cornstarch	2 tablespoons dry sherry
2 tablespoons water	1/2 cup Quick Beef Broth, page 133,
2 tablespoons soy sauce	or Vegetable Broth, page 133

In a small bowl, stir cornstarch into water. Stir in soy sauce, sherry and broth. Makes about 3/4 cup.

Worcestershire-Lemon Sauce

1 teaspoon cornstarch	1/2 cup Quick Beef Broth, page 133,
1 tablespoon Worcestershire sauce	or Vegetable Broth, page 133
1 tablespoon lemon juice	

In a small bowl, stir cornstarch into Worcestershire sauce. Stir in lemon juice and broth. Makes about 3/4 cup.

Hoisin Steak Sauce

1 teaspoon cornstarch	2 tablespoons rice wine or brandy
2 tablespoons water	1/2 cup Quick Beef Broth, page 133,
2 teaspoons hoisin sauce	or Vegetable Broth, page 133

In a small bowl, stir cornstarch into water. Stir in hoisin sauce, rice wine or brandy and broth. Makes about 1/2 cup.

Sauce Diable

1 lb. minced green onions	1 teaspoon Worcestershire sauce
1/4 cup dry white wine	1 teaspoon Dijon-style mustard
1 (7-oz.) can brown beef gravy	1 tablespoon butter
2 tablespoons brandy	Salt and pepper to taste

Combine green onions and wine in a large saucepan. Simmer over low heat until liquid has almost evaporated. Add remaining ingredients. Bring to a gentle boil. Makes about 2 cups.

Mustard Sauce

1 tablespoon Dijon-style mustard	2 tablespoons butter
1 (7-oz.) can brown beef gravy	

Combine ingredients in a small saucepan. Stir over low heat until butter melts and sauce is hot. Makes about 1 cup.

Desserts

How can I start a book with the promise that you can maintain or regain a trim, slim figure by cooking with a wok and end with a chapter of scrumptious desserts? Easy. Most of these desserts are lower in calories than those you'll find in the average cookbook. But they are not intended as diet desserts. Far from it. People everywhere deserve a few happy endings, a little sweet in their life. These desserts are just that—sweet and happy endings to almost any meal.

Each recipe was developed especially for the wok. Why turn on the oven, which uses more fuel and heats up the entire kitchen, when the wok is available? Desserts should be beautiful, and indeed, these are. They are also easy to prepare and fail-proof. You can make them with confidence and serve them with pride.

Wok-cooked desserts vary from light and airy to rich and compact. Jewel-like, glittering Holiday Meringue Cake is much lower in calories than fruitcake. It's just the dessert to please everyone after an old-fashioned turkey-with-all-the-trimmings meal. Stained-Glass Peaches are the perfect choice when it's your turn to have the bridge club for lunch. They give only 50 calories per serving. Or you can serve Down-East Poppy Seed Cake, which is especially nice with mid-morning coffee or afternoon tea.

I've always said that nothing could top my favorite Manhattan-style cheesecake, but now I take it back. Velvet-smooth Tofu Cheesecake is fabulous, and it's low-calorie. Try all of the desserts. You can always serve a dessert when low-calorie stir-fried or steamed dishes are the main course. ❖

Dessert & Coffee Party

Peppermint Meringue Cake, page 142
Stained-Glass Peaches, page 147
Orange Upside-Down Cake, page 150
Tofu Cheesecake, page 151
Coffee
Sweetened Whipped Cream or Brandy

Pink-Cloud Meringue Cake

A beautiful, light and airy dessert.

1 tablespoon sugar for Bundt pan
9 egg whites
1 teaspoon strawberry-flavor gelatin powder
1/2 teaspoon vanilla extract or
almond extract

1 cup plus 2 tablespoons sugar
1 pint fresh strawberries, hulled
2 tablespoons currant jelly

Butter a 12-cup Bundt pan. Sprinkle with 1 tablespoon sugar, tipping pan to distribute evenly; set aside. In a large bowl, beat egg whites until frothy. Sprinkle gelatin evenly over surface of beaten egg whites. Add vanilla or almond extract. Add sugar 1 tablespoon at a time, beating thoroughly after each addition. Continue beating until mixture forms stiff, glossy peaks. Spoon into prepared pan. Use a spatula to remove any large air holes and to smooth top. Place a rack in wok. Pour water into wok until 1 inch below rack. Bring to a gentle boil over medium heat. Place pan on rack. Cover wok; steam 30 minutes. Add boiling water to wok, if needed. Steam cake 15 minutes longer or until top feels dry when touched with your fingertips. Cool 5 minutes on a rack. Cake will shrink about 1 inch. Invert pan and cake onto a serving plate. Remove pan. Refrigerate 1 hour or until chilled. To serve, fill center of cake with strawberries. Cut large berries in half. In a small saucepan, melt jelly. Spoon over berries. Makes 8 servings.

Peppermint Meringue Cake

Two of my favorite flavors combined in a beautiful fantasy cake.

1 tablespoon sugar for Bundt pan
1-1/4 cups sugar
1/4 cup lime-flavor gelatin powder
9 egg whites

1/2 teaspoon peppermint flavoring
1 (7-1/4-oz.) pkg. chocolate hard-shell
topping

Butter a 12-cup Bundt pan. Sprinkle with 1 tablespoon sugar, tipping pan to distribute evenly; set aside. In a small bowl, combine 1-1/4 cups sugar and gelatin; set aside. In a large bowl, use electric mixer to beat egg whites and peppermint flavoring until frothy. Add sugar mixture, 1/4 cup at a time, beating well after each addition. Continue beating until mixture forms stiff, glossy peaks. Spoon into prepared pan. Use a spatula to remove air holes and to smooth top. Place a rack in wok. Pour water into wok until 1 inch below rack. Bring to a gentle boil over medium heat. Place pan on rack. Cover wok. Steam 30 minutes. Add boiling water to wok, if needed. Steam cake 15 minutes longer or until top of cake feels dry to touch. Cool cake on a cooling rack. Cake will shrink about 1 inch. Invert pan and cake onto a serving plate. Remove pan. Refrigerate 1 hour or until chilled. Drizzle with chocolate hard-shell topping. Refrigerate cake until served. Makes 8 servings.

Pink-Cloud Meringue Cake

Mocha Angel Cake

Light but rich.

3/4 cup cake flour
3/4 cup powdered sugar
1/4 cup unsweetened cocoa powder
2 tablespoons instant coffee powder
9 large egg whites

1-1/2 teaspoons cream of tartar
1 teaspoon rum extract
1 cup sifted powdered sugar
Rum Glaze, see below

Rum Glaze:
2 tablespoons butter, melted, hot
3 tablespoons light rum

1-1/2 to 2 cups sifted powdered sugar

Sift flour with 3/4 cup powdered sugar, cocoa powder and coffee powder; set aside. In a large bowl, combine egg whites, cream of tartar and rum extract. Beat with electric mixer on medium speed until frothy. Gradually beat in 1 cup sifted powdered sugar 2 tablespoons at a time, beating well after each addition. Continue to beat at high speed until stiff peaks form. Using a rubber spatula, gently fold in flour mixture, a fourth at a time. Fold only until flour mixture is distributed. Spoon into an ungreased 9-inch tube pan or 12-cup Bundt pan. Place a rack in wok. Pour water into wok until 1 inch below rack. Bring water to a gentle boil over medium heat. Place pan on rack. Cover wok; steam 30 minutes. Lift lid slightly and quickly add boiling water, if needed. Steam 30 minutes longer or until center of cake springs back when lightly touched with your fingertips. Invert cake in pan over a cooling rack. Cool to room temperature. Use the blade of a metal spatula to loosen cake from pan. Invert onto a serving plate. Remove pan. Prepare Rum Glaze. Spoon over top of cake. Makes 8 servings.

Rum Glaze:
In a small bowl, beat butter, rum and powdered sugar until smooth. Makes about 3/4 cup.

Easy Pears Hélène

A very easy and delicious version of a classic French dessert.

1-1/2 oz. semisweet baking chocolate
6 or 8 canned pear halves, drained

2 tablespoons light rum
4 scoops vanilla ice cream

Grate chocolate using coarse side of hand grater or electric food processor. Place pears, cut side down, in single layer in an 8-inch round glass baking dish. Pour rum equally over each pear. Place a rack in wok. Pour water into wok until 1 inch below rack. Bring to a gentle boil over medium heat. Place dish on rack. Cover wok; steam 5 minutes. Sprinkle each pear with grated chocolate. Steam about 1 minute longer until chocolate is melted. Cool dish on a rack 15 minutes. Place slightly cooled pears in refrigerator until chocolate hardens, about 30 minutes. To serve, place a scoop of ice cream in each of 4 dessert dishes. Place 2 pear halves, chocolate side up, on top of each scoop. Makes 4 servings.

Lemon Angel

This light and lemony angel-food cake has a sparkling crystal glaze.

1 cup sifted cake flour	1-1/2 teaspoons lemon extract
3/4 cup sifted powdered sugar	1/4 teaspoon salt
10 egg whites	1 cup sifted powdered sugar
1/2 teaspoon cream of tartar	Orange Crystal Glaze, see below

Orange Crystal Glaze:

1 cup sugar	3 tablespoons lemon juice
6 tablespoons orange juice	1/4 cup orange liqueur, if desired

Sift flour with 3/4 cup powdered sugar; set aside. In a large bowl, beat egg whites with cream of tartar, lemon extract and salt until soft peaks form. Add 1 cup powdered sugar, 2 tablespoons at a time, beating well after each addition. Continue to beat at high speed until stiff peaks form. Using a rubber spatula, gently fold in flour mixture, 1/4 cup at a time. Spoon into an ungreased 9-inch tube pan. Place a rack in wok. Pour water into wok until 1 inch below rack. Bring to a gentle boil over medium heat. Place tube pan on rack. Cover wok; steam 30 minutes. Lift lid slightly and quickly add boiling water to raise level of water to 1 inch below rack. Replace cover. Steam 30 minutes longer or until center springs back when lightly touched with your fingertips. Invert cake in pan on counter. Cool to room temperature. While cake steams, prepare Orange Crystal Glaze; set aside. Use a metal spatula to loosen cake from side of pan. Turn out onto a serving plate. Stir Orange Crystal Glaze. Spoon over surface of cake. Makes 8 servings.

Orange Crystal Glaze:

In small bowl, blend all ingredients. Stirring occasionally, let stand 1 hour. Sugar will only partially dissolve. Makes about 1 cup.

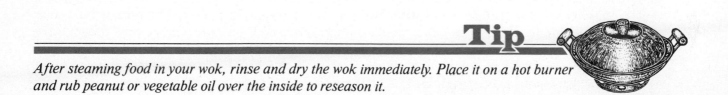

Tip

After steaming food in your wok, rinse and dry the wok immediately. Place it on a hot burner and rub peanut or vegetable oil over the inside to reseason it.

Banana Fritters

Tastes like Bananas Foster.

Orange-Apricot Sauce, see below
16 won ton skins
2 small bananas, coarsely chopped

1 tablespoon lemon juice
2 tablespoons brown sugar
Oil for deep-frying

Orange-Apricot Sauce:
1/2 cup apricot jam
2 tablespoons sugar
1/2 cup orange juice
2 teaspoons cornstarch

2 tablespoons water
1 tablespoon orange liqueur or
  2 tablespoons sugar plus 2 or
  3 drops orange extract

Prepare Orange-Apricot Sauce. Set aside; keep warm. To keep skins from drying out, prepare only 6 fritters at a time. Keep fritters and skins covered with a damp cloth until ready to fry. In a small bowl, toss bananas with lemon juice and brown sugar. Arrange 6 won ton skins on a flat surface. Spoon 1 tablespoon banana mixture onto center of each skin. Brush edges of skins with water. Fold over filling to form triangles. Press edges together to seal. Pour oil for deep-frying into wok until 1-1/2 inches deep in center. Heat oil to 350F (175C). Fry 2 or 3 fritters at a time in hot oil until golden brown. Drain on paper towels. Top with Orange-Apricot Sauce. Makes 16 fritters.

Orange-Apricot Sauce:
In a small saucepan, combine apricot jam, 2 tablespoons sugar and orange juice. Stir over low heat until sugar dissolves and mixture is hot. In a small bowl, combine cornstarch and water. Stir into orange juice mixture until thickened. Remove from heat. Stir in orange liqueur or sugar and orange extract. Serve warm or at room temperature. Makes about 1 cup.

Candy-Store Apples

As glittering and irresistible as a Christmas tree.

4 cooking apples
1/2 cup water
About 1-1/2 cups red cinnamon candy
1/2 cup light rum

Rock crystal candy, if desired
3 to 4 tablespoons sugar
Thin, shiny peppermint-stick candy

Peel apples about 2/3 of way down from blossom end. Cut out and discard core. Arrange cored apples, stem end down, in an 8-inch square glass baking dish. Pour water into dish. Fill centers of apples with cinnamon candies. Pour rum over candies, letting rum overflow onto apples. Scatter a few cinnamon candies in bottom of dish. Place a rack in wok. Pour water into wok until 1 inch below rack. Bring to a gentle boil over medium heat. Place dish on rack. Cover wok. Steam until apples are tender enough to cut with a dessert spoon, 15 to 20 minutes. Cool slightly. Refrigerate until chilled, about 1 hour. To serve, place each apple on an individual dessert plate and surround with rock crystal candy, if desired. Drizzle cooking liquid over candy. Before serving, shake sugar through a small sieve over tops and sides of each apple. Fill centers with more cinnamon candies. Place 1 long and 1 short candy peppermint stick in each apple. Makes 4 servings.

How to Make Stained-Glass Peaches

1/Place peach halves, cut side down, in an 8-inch round glass baking dish. Sprinkle with brown sugar and rum.

2/Sprinkle each flavor gelatin in a random design over surface of steamed peaches.

Stained-Glass Peaches

As spectacular to look at as they are delicious to eat.

6 fresh peaches or 12 canned peach halves
Boiling water
2 tablespoons light brown sugar
2 tablespoons light or dark rum

1 tablespoon strawberry-flavor or
　　cherry-flavor gelatin powder
1 tablespoon lime-flavor gelatin powder
1 tablespoon orange-flavor gelatin powder

Plunge fresh peaches into a pot of boiling water, 1 at a time. Hold hot peaches under cold, running water and slip skins off. Cut peeled peaches in half and remove seeds. If using canned peaches, drain on paper towels. Place peach halves, cut side down, in an 8-inch round glass baking dish. Sprinkle with brown sugar and rum. Place a rack in wok. Pour water into wok until 1 inch below rack. Bring to a gentle boil over medium heat. Place dish on rack. Cover wok. Steam fresh peaches until tender enough to pierce easily with tines of a fork, 5 to 8 minutes. Steam canned peaches until sugar dissolves, 3 to 4 minutes. Remove dish from wok. Sprinkle surface of peaches with each flavor gelatin in a random design. Makes 6 servings.

Variation

Substitute a mixture of fruits for peaches.

Tropical-Fruits Flambé

A spectacular finale for a party meal and a grand way to use your wok.

2 navel oranges
1 crisp tart apple, peeled, coarsely chopped
1 ripe pear, peeled, coarsely chopped
1 kiwi, peeled, thinly sliced
1 banana, peeled, cut in thick slices
1/4 cup sugar

3 tablespoons light rum or brandy
1/4 cup light rum or brandy
4 or 6 scoops vanilla ice cream
1/4 cup butter
1/2 cup sugar

Using a small sharp knife, cut oranges into quarters. Cut quarters into thick wedges. Holding each orange wedge over a medium bowl, cut fruit from peel into bowl. Discard peel. Add apple, pear, kiwi and banana. Sprinkle with 1/4 cup sugar and 3 tablespoons rum or brandy. Let stand at least 30 minutes at room temperature. Pour 1/4 cup rum or brandy into a small pitcher. Place pitcher in pan of boiling water. Let stand 5 minutes to warm. To prepare at serving table, assemble all ingredients. Place each scoop of ice cream in separate dessert dishes. Melt butter in wok over medium-high heat. When it begins to foam, add fruit mixture. Stir-fry until just heated, about 1 minute. Sprinkle with 1/2 cup sugar. Remove from heat. Immediately pour warmed rum or brandy over fruit mixture. Ignite with a long-handled match. Let flame burn until it goes out. Ladle fruit mixture over ice cream. Serve immediately. Makes 4 or 6 servings.

Huguenot Tart

This wok version of an old Charleston recipe is even better than the original.

2 large eggs
1 cup sugar
3/4 cup all-purpose flour
1 teaspoon baking powder
1 teaspoon ground cinnamon
1/2 teaspoon ground nutmeg
1/4 teaspoon ground cloves

1 teaspoon coarsely ground black pepper
1 cup finely chopped, peeled tart apples
3/4 cup chopped walnuts
1/4 cup raisins
1 teaspoon vanilla extract
Sweetened whipped cream or
    vanilla ice cream

Lightly butter an 8-inch square glass baking dish; set aside. In a medium ovenproof bowl, combine eggs and sugar. Place over, but not in, a pan of simmering water. Beat egg mixture with electric mixer or wire whisk until sugar has dissolved and mixture has doubled in volume. Remove bowl from pan. Sift together flour, baking powder, cinnamon, nutmeg, cloves and pepper. Fold flour mixture into egg mixture. Fold in apples, walnuts and raisins. Stir in vanilla. Spoon batter into prepared baking dish. Place a rack in wok. Pour water into wok until 1 inch below rack. Bring water to a gentle boil over medium heat. Place dish on rack. Loosely cover dish with foil. Cover wok; steam 30 minutes. Cool tart in dish on a cooling rack, 10 minutes. Cut cooled tart into squares. Use a spatula to place squares on individual plates. Serve warm or at room temperature. Top each serving with sweetened whipped cream or ice cream. Makes 6 servings.

Orange-Cheese Pie

Pie in a wok? Yes indeed! Creamy smooth and sinfully rich.

1/3 cup butter	2 tablespoons orange marmalade
1-1/4 cups fine, dry chocolate-wafer crumbs	2 tablespoons orange liqueur
2 (8-oz.) pkgs. cream cheese, warmed	1 cup dairy sour cream
1/3 cup granulated sugar	2 tablespoons brown sugar
2 eggs	2 navel oranges

Butter a 9-inch pie plate; set aside. Melt 1/3 cup butter in a small skillet. Stir in crumbs. Press crumb mixture over bottom and up side of pie plate; set aside. In a medium bowl, beat cream cheese until fluffy. Gradually beat in 1/3 cup granulated sugar until blended. Add eggs 1 at a time, beating well after each addition. Fold in orange marmalade and liqueur. Spoon mixture evenly over crumbs. Place a rack in wok. Pour water into wok until 1 inch below rack. Bring to a gentle boil over medium heat. Place pie plate on rack. Cover loosely with foil. Cover wok; steam 30 minutes. In a small bowl, combine sour cream and brown sugar. Spread evenly over surface of steamed pie. Steam 5 minutes longer. Cool on a rack 5 minutes. Refrigerate 1 hour or until chilled. Peel oranges, removing white pith. Cut peeled oranges into thin slices. Cut each slice into 4 wedges. Arrange orange wedges over top of pie. Serve chilled. Makes 6 to 8 servings.

Cherry-Cheese Pie

One of the surest ways you'll find to make your reputation as a fabulous dessert cook.

No-Bake Graham-Cracker Crust, see below	2 eggs
1 (8-oz.) pkg. cream cheese, softened	2 teaspoons grated lemon peel
1/2 cup sugar	1 (16-oz.) can cherry-pie filling
1/2 cup mayonnaise	

No-Bake Graham-Cracker Crust:
1/4 cup butter, softened
1-1/4 cups graham-cracker crumbs

Prepare No-Bake Graham-Cracker Crust. Refrigerate until chilled and firm, about 30 minutes. In a large bowl, combine cream cheese, sugar, mayonnaise, eggs and lemon peel. Gently beat with electric mixer on low speed or with a wire whisk only until blended. Pour into prepared crust. Place a rack in wok. Pour water into wok until 1 inch below rack. Bring to a gentle boil over medium heat. Place pie plate on rack. Cover wok. Steam 25 to 30 minutes until knife inserted in center comes out clean. Cool on a rack. Top with cherry pie filling. Makes 8 servings.

No-Bake Graham-Cracker Crust:
In a small saucepan, melt butter over low heat. Stir in crumbs until blended. Spread mixture over bottom and up side of a 9-inch pie plate.

Tofu Cheesecake

This cheesecake is a fabulous low-calorie dessert.

3 tablespoons butter
1 cup graham-cracker crumbs
1 (15-1/4-oz.) can pineapple chunks in pineapple juice
2 eggs
1/2 cup sugar

1/2 teaspoon vanilla extract
1/2 teaspoon grated lemon peel
8 oz. tofu, crumbled
1 (8-oz.) pkg. Neufchâtel cheese
1/2 cup vanilla-flavor yogurt
Maraschino cherries for garnish

In a small saucepan, melt butter over low heat. Stir in graham-cracker crumbs. Press crumb mixture over bottom and up side of a 9-inch pie plate. Refrigerate until firm. Drain pineapple, reserving juice in blender or food processor. Set pineapple aside. Add eggs, sugar, vanilla and lemon peel to juice. Process 2 to 3 seconds. If using food processor, add tofu and Neufchâtel cheese. Blend until smooth. If using blender, add half of tofu and half of Neufchâtel cheese. Blend until smooth. Add remaining tofu and cheese. Blend until smooth. Pour tofu mixture into chilled crust. Place a rack in wok. Pour water into wok until 1 inch below rack. Bring to a gentle boil over medium heat. Place pie plate on rack. Cover wok. Steam 30 minutes or until a knife inserted in center comes out clean. Cool on a rack 3 minutes. Spread vanilla yogurt over cooked tofu mixture. Garnish with drained pineapple chunks and maraschino cherries. Refrigerate 30 minutes or until chilled. Makes 8 servings.

Omelets Alaska

The wok lets you keep an even, high heat for this easily prepared gourmet dessert.

About 1/2 cup vanilla ice cream
4 teaspoons cornstarch
1/4 cup light rum or dry sherry
4 extra-large eggs, slightly beaten

About 1 teaspoon oil
1/4 cup butter
Powdered sugar

Remove ice cream from freezer to soften slightly. Cut four 4-inch squares of waxed paper. Spoon about 2 tablespoons ice cream onto 1 piece of waxed paper. Roll ice cream in waxed paper, making a 1-1/2-inch cylinder, about 1/2-inch in diameter. Place on a flat metal tray or on foil. Repeat with remaining ice cream and waxed paper. Place in freezer until firm, 1 to 2 hours. In a small bowl, combine cornstarch and rum or sherry. Beat until smooth. Beat in eggs until blended; set aside. Place wok on high heat. Add a few drops of oil. With a piece of paper towel, spread oil evenly over bottom and up side of wok. Add 1 tablespoon butter. Heat until bubbly. Beat egg mixture again to blend. Pour a fourth of egg mixture into wok. Tilt wok back and forth to spread mixture evenly over bottom and slightly up side of wok. Cook, without stirring, until top of omelet is almost dry. Remove paper from 1 ice cream roll. Place ice cream a little off-center on side away from you. Quickly fold omelet over ice cream. Tilt wok away from you. Using a metal spatula, quickly lift omelet from wok to a serving plate. Sprinkle with powdered sugar. Serve immediately. Repeat with remaining ingredients. Makes 4 servings.

Caribbean Mardi-Gras Pudding

Luscious tropical flavor.

2 tablespoons finely chopped nuts
1/2 cup butter, room temperature
1/2 cup orange juice, room temperature
1 whole egg, room temperature
1 egg yolk, room temperature
3/4 cup packed brown sugar
1/2 cup graham cracker crumbs

1 cup all-purpose flour
1/2 teaspoon baking powder
1/2 teaspoon baking soda
1 (8-oz.) can crushed pineapple
2 tablespoons orange marmalade
Orange-Pineapple Glaze, see below

Orange-Pineapple Glaze:
3/4 cup orange marmalade
2 tablespoons brandy or lemon juice

Generously butter an 8-inch square glass baking dish. Sprinkle side and bottom with chopped nuts. In a large bowl, combine remaining ingredients except for Orange-Pineapple Glaze. Beat with electric mixer on medium speed 2 minutes, scraping bowl often. Place a rack in wok. Pour water into wok until 1 inch below rack. Bring water to a gentle boil over medium heat. Place dish on rack. Cover wok. Steam 45 minutes or until center of cake springs back when lightly pressed with your fingertips. Add boiling water to wok as needed. Place dish on a rack to cool 10 minutes. Prepare Orange-Pineapple Glaze. Set aside and keep hot. Invert cooled cake onto a serving plate. Remove dish. Puncture cake 12 to 15 times with a skewer or small knife. Slowly pour hot glaze over warm cake. Spoon glaze from plate onto cake until liquid is absorbed. Makes 12 servings.

Orange-Pineapple Glaze:
In small saucepan, combine marmalade and brandy or lemon juice. Stir over medium heat until marmalade is melted but still thick. Makes about 3/4 cup.

Pillow-Puff Cookies

Another really great way to make use of versatile won ton skins.

24 won ton skins
1/2 cup chopped walnuts, pecans or peanuts
1/2 cup shredded or flaked coconut
About 2 tablespoons honey

Water
Oil for deep frying
Powdered sugar

In a small bowl, combine nuts and coconut. Add enough honey to hold mixture together. On center of 1 won ton skin, spoon 1 tablespoon nut mixture. Use a pastry brush or your fingers to moisten edges of skin with water. Top with a second won ton skin. Press edges firmly together to seal. Prepare 6 filled cookies at a time for frying. Keep won ton skins and shaped cookies covered with a damp cloth until ready to fry. Pour oil for deep-frying into wok until 1-1/2 inches deep in center. Heat oil to 350F (175C). Fry 2 or 3 filled cookies a few at a time in hot oil. Fry until puffed and golden brown, about 1 minute. Drain on paper towels. Sprinkle with powdered sugar. Repeat with remaining won ton skins and filling. Makes 12 cookies.

____ How to Make Butterfly Cinnamon Cookies ____

1/Cut a 1-1/4-inch slit through both triangles, 1/2 inch from, and parallel to, cut edge. Pull points through slit.

2/Fry won ton butterflies in hot oil, 2 or 3 at a time. Drain on paper towels. Sprinkle with cinnamon-sugar mixture.

Butterfly Cinnamon Cookies

You'll have fun making this cookie.

1 cup powdered sugar
1 tablespoon cinnamon

24 won ton skins
Oil for deep-frying

Sift powdered sugar with cinnamon; set aside. Keep won ton skins and shaped skins covered with a damp cloth. Shape and fry 6 skins at a time. Cut 1 won ton skin in half diagonally, making 2 triangles. Place 1 triangle on top of other triangle. Cut a 1-1/4-inch slit through both triangles, 1/2 inch from, and parallel to, cut edge. Pull points from one end through slit. Repeat until 6 won ton skins have been shaped. Pour oil for deep-frying into wok until 1-1/2 inches deep in center. Heat oil to 350F (175C). Fry won ton butterflies in hot oil, 2 or 3 at a time. Drain on paper towels. Sprinkle with cinnamon-sugar mixture. Cool on a rack. Repeat with remaining won ton skins, preparing 6 at a time. Makes 24 cookies.

Index

8.78223752172230